Be Aware

By

Tina Cornish

Be Aware

Copyright © 2016 by Tina Cornish

Artwork copyright © 2016 Tina Cornish (Cover, images 1, 9, 10 & 11).
With permission, artwork copyright © 2016 Tiela Rabie (images 2 – 8).
Certain names have been changed to protect identities.
Independently published by Tina Cornish www.tinacornish.co.za
ISBN: 978-0-620-72212-4

Dedication

This book is dedicated to all of you.

For those who have asked, "How do you do it?" or "How do you change and just know?", 'Be Aware' is one of those guides for you to become consciously aware. While creation of this book has been a gift and a guide in my journey of life, I sincerely wish it to be a vehicle through which you may find your own gifts and transform your life.

Tina Cornish

Contents

Acknowledgements

Thank you to everyone who was involved in assisting my process of healing and transformation, and all who have been in contact with me during my life.

Thanks to God, all my Spirit Guides, Masters, Archangels, and Guardian Angels for their guidance and assistance in memory recall and healing.

Thanks to my children, Casey-Jean and Dustin, for all your love, patience and understanding while I lavishly spent time in writing and healing. For all your parenting lessons you brought forward for me. I pray my book makes a positive difference in your lives.

Thanks to my parents David and Colleen; for having raised me with an open view to life and religions, allowing me to choose my own way of belief; for guiding and parenting me in the best way they knew how.

Thanks to my ex-husband, for all the love we shared; the fun, the laughter, the joy, the sharing of his Soul; the challenges and lessons that guided me towards creating an interdependent relationship; for teaching me to not become attached and dependent on another for love, but to rather search for the love within. Each and every one of those moments re-awakened me further to knowing WHO I AM, and igniting my full divine power. I will always be grateful for what you guided forth, assisting my transformation during our time together.

My immense gratitude goes to my long-standing doctor. He has always gone far and beyond his call of duty with his incredible patience, understanding, and caring; his amazing sense of humour that always lifted my spirits when, through illness, I was down and disappointed. Through it all, I was unaware of the blessings, training and guidance I was undergoing for my Soul purpose. A doctor who has always given me the freedom to express my feelings truthfully and, whenever necessary, to help me heal in my own way; having always given me his undivided attention; a doctor, who became my mentor, having taught and led me, by example, how to be both empathetic and professional with patients.

Thanks to Tiela Rabie, for her amazing, tailored artwork in this book, bringing in her own wonderful sense of humour; and, especially, for being the teacher, Reiki Master and friend to assist my healing journey.

Thanks to my husband, Martin Cornish. I am so grateful you have come into my life and given me both experience and proof of a loving, positive, supportive and respectful relationship. It is such a joy to give and receive so many loving hugs.

Tina Cornish

Introduction - How To Use This Book

'Be Aware' is written to teach, guide and inspire you to move forward into your own conscious healing moments and transform your life. Allow yourself to 'Be Aware' and present in your own life. Feel your emotions, listen to and acknowledge your thoughts, and connect with your body. Learn how to heal yourself through your own path of self-discovery. Have a journal or pad of paper and a pen beside you while reading to write down your own thoughts and feelings relating to your life. This book will become a trigger for your transformation and healing in your life. 'Be Aware' is held within the Christ-lighted, higher dimensional energy to help you shift for your own highest good, in whatever way you may need it in the present.

Be an observer throughout section one as I take you on my journey, my personal thoughts and feelings. Allow yourself to go 'behind the scenes' of a developing, healing consciousness. Take note of my drive towards changing my negative and debilitating thoughts to positive, constructive ones. See how everyday life, everyday events and everyday happenings are important healing moments for you to experience.

At times we are confused. It is a lack of awareness and understanding of our own life patterns that create this confusion. Together with the universe, we subconsciously create our own lessons for transformation. See how I attracted people and events, and experienced emotions, to teach myself lessons that would, in turn, be used to enhance my own progress. Sometimes it is important in one's life to surrender and release situations for healing to occur. Trust implicitly that the universe will re-align you with awareness of your Soul-pathway. You too may find moments in your life when you become aware that you have knowledge of events along your pathway even *before* they take place. Accept them as guidance and preparation and, using your own discernment, keep yourself inspired.

If you haven't already read any of Louise L. Hay's books or attended any of her workshops, *now* would be a good time. You can relate much of my healing interpretation to her teachings. I recommend her book 'Heal Your Body', from which you will get in-depth knowledge of the metaphysical healing connection between body, mind and spirit. My own healing interpretations, based on the concept of metaphysical causation-or how words and thoughts can create lived experiences-and combined with Louise L. Hay's interpretations, (at the end of each chapter from my life), will connect some of the missing pieces. This is where the healing journey unfolds while my life transforms. It shows you a way in which you too can review your life. It could be very useful for you to have 'Heal Your Body' on hand while you read 'Be Aware', as your own memories of illness may come to light.

This book is about my 'Soul' life through many lifetimes. Some thoughts from past lives emerge in my current life. It doesn't really matter in which life the events took place. All that matters is that my Soul has gone through experiences and healing and my life has transformed naturally. Learn how useful recall of past events will help to heal you in your current life. I see life as a puzzle of a million pieces, waiting for the divine moment to fit together perfectly to bring unique healing experiences into your life. Some healing, perhaps from the same event or trauma, may unfold at different intervals in your life. Like pages in a book, they bring to your awareness something new, while at the same time taking you to a different level of healing and transformation. Learn to go with the flow to experience it. Don't run and hide, as I first tried to do; that only holds up your healing progress. Learn to see the blessings in the experiences and, especially, the problems.

Know that during the reading of this book you may notice your own emotions being stirred. You may feel a connection to me in some way. One reason for this is the energy field within which this book is held. This will help you to heal and transform for your highest good. You have attracted this book to you. If emotions arise, this is telling you that energies are shifting within you and healing is automatically taking place. I advise you then to put the book aside and work through whatever is developing within you. Write down your thoughts and feelings and allow yourself to express your emotions. Don't hold back or ignore them because this suppresses the energy and this, in turn, may lead to further illnesses or blocks in your life. Seize your moment of healing and transformation! After you have worked through this, return to re-reading the section that first triggered your release. You may need to repeat this a number of times, depending on your circumstances. An indication that healing has occurred is that no further emotions are triggered. Remember that anger is also an emotion, a blanket suppressing a deeper hurt. Also, pay attention to areas you may want to reject and go within: ask what your reason for rejection truly is. We often think we have dealt with our past effectively, but we merely succeed in blocking and suppressing emotion and trauma temporarily, not wanting to return consciously to a sad or depressing event. A sure sign of withheld energies from your past would be illnesses you may have experienced or problems you may have attracted, as well as the emotions connected to the memories. Looking carefully at some of the illnesses in your past can reveal and also release a 'pattern' hidden deep within you. If you have experienced any major traumatic event in your life, you may find yourself feeling strangely depressed during the reading of my book. Have a box of tissues handy! Always seek professional help if you feel unable to deal with the rising emotions. You are most welcome to contact me too for further help. Focus on lifting yourself into a positive vibration after you release any emotions to prevent yourself becoming immersed in depression. You can do this by congratulating yourself and giving yourself a hug for having the courage and strength to go back into the experience of the emotions and memories. Avoid following a chain of negative thoughts that may keep surfacing. You are the only one who can change that negative thought. The quickest way to dispel confusion is to know and to trust that everything you go through is absolutely necessary for your progress and growth. When you do this, the 'puzzle pieces of your life' will start falling into place perfectly. You will 'Be Aware'. Simply by becoming more in touch with your thoughts and feelings, your awareness will begin to shift, healing of some sort will take place and you will feel the freedom and peace that follows. My book does not at all imply that Reiki is the only pathway to healing, transformation and ascension. It is not. You must follow your own guided pathway and healing modality from within you.

What Is Reiki Healing?

The power and discipline behind Reiki healing (pronounced Ray-Key)

Reiki is a totally safe and natural energy healing modality. It originates from Japan and uses the natural universal life force energy that supports all of creation. Reiki was re-discovered by a Japanese Christian man, Dr Mikao Usui, in the 1800s and has over the years been passed down from Reiki Master to student through sacred teachings, healings and attunements. Reiki is practised more often in the form of 'hands-on' treatments, but does extend into distant healing. One can relate Reiki to the natural, powerful and loving touch we all use when interacting through a state of unconditional love towards another: the natural ability within us when we reach out lovingly to touch a new-born baby, or to comfort our child through touch when they have hurt themselves. The touch is often empowered by saying "let me rub that better for you".

Reiki Masters and Practitioners have undergone specific teachings, cleansings, self-healing treatments, experiences and attunements. These purify and uplift their energy fields into a positive vibration of energy, to enable their becoming an open conduit. During attunements, sacred symbols are passed to the student, by the Master. During a treatment the Reiki Practitioner or Master will use these symbols where necessary to enhance and uplift the energies required by your body. The symbols greatly empower the universal life force energy, creating a specific, higher, and more positive vibration of energy. It is these symbols that give Reiki its uniqueness. The Reiki Master or Practitioner does not heal you. He or she is purely a trained channel through which the higher positive vibration of energies may be passed to you. Your body will absorb the energy and use it in its own magnificent manner, in accordance with your Soul. This then brings about the necessary healing, through shifting and changing your energy vibrations. Reiki works on all levels of your being and can therefore help to heal all illnesses or traumas, minor or major. Reiki can be, and often is, integrated into other healing modalities.

Be Aware

Your typical Reiki treatment lasts 30 to 60 minutes. You remain fully clothed while relaxing on a treatment bed. The more relaxed you are, the greater the ability of your body to let go and accept these divine energies. The Reiki Master and Practitioner are trained to follow certain hand positions aligned with your chakras. The chakras are energy vortices emanating from your physical body into your aura. They are absorbing energy at all times during your life and developing their vibrational signature in cycles of seven year periods. The Master or Practitioner will intuitively follow their own guidance and senses to assist in removing energy blockages that can often be felt, or seen, within the aura. During the treatment you might experience mild relaxation, or a deeper state such as meditation, even a peaceful sleep. Energy flows through the Master or Practitioner the moment their hands are gently placed on your body or within any part of your aura. During the transference of energy you may feel your Master's or Practitioner's hands vibrating with a flood of warm, tingling sensations. It is also quite common for the hand temperature of the Master or Practitioner to change from hot to cold, directly connected to your own unique needs. Throughout life, your chakras and body are energetically developing as they absorb all your experiences. Your body does not differentiate between positive and negative experiences; when energies from traumatic experiences build up, they leave an energy imprint within the chakra or a part of your body. Over time this can, and often does, develop into illness, as well as repeated illnesses of the same kind. When the Master or Practitioner carries out a healing treatment, the higher energy is absorbed and your body begins to realign itself. It lets go of negative, low vibrations and traumas, replacing them with higher, positive vibrations. While this happens you may experience tingling of the skin, itchiness, pulling of muscles and slight jerking as your energy re-balances. It often passes quite quickly. On a mental level you can experience spontaneous flashes of colour or visualisations, as well as a flood of suppressed memories. This often triggers a release of emotions, opening you to greater awareness.

Be Aware

After your treatment you are usually given a glass of healing water to drink. This is water that has been purified and uplifted through Reiki into a higher vibration of energy. You are encouraged to continue drinking more water within the next 24 hours as this aids absorption of the higher vibrational frequencies into your blood, cleansing and releasing toxins.

You may experience an increase in vitality and positive thought patterns after a treatment, providing you with more harmony, serenity, clear thinking and focus. This leads to attracting more positive experiences into your life. Regular treatments will increase the strength of your energy field and help prevent illness.

Reiki is not limited to humans and is very often used in the healing of animals and all that exists in creation. Reiki is governed through the discipline of the following five principles, originally set in place by Dr Usui.

Just for today I will live the attitude of gratitude
Just for today I will not worry
Just for today I will not anger
Just for today I will do my work honestly
Just for today I will show love and respect for every living thing

Chakra Colours and Development Cycle

1. Base Root Chakra – Red – years 1-7 & 49-56
2. Sacral Chakra – Orange – years 7-14 & 56-63
3. Solar Plexus Chakra – Yellow – years 14-21 & 63-70
4. Heart Chakra – Green/Pink – years 21-28 & 70-77
5. Throat Chakra – Blue – years 28-35 & 77-84
6. Brow/3rd Eye Chakra – Indigo – years 35-42 & 84-91
7. Crown Chakra – Violet/white – years 42-49 & 91-98

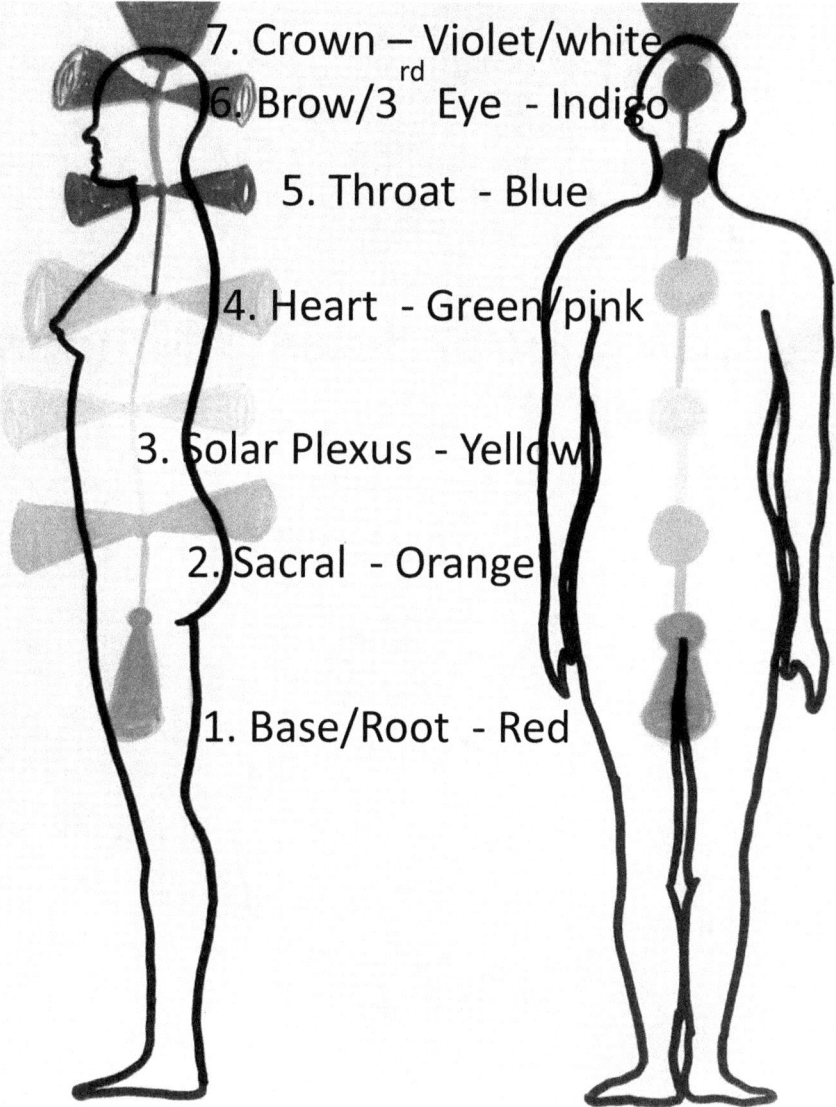

7. Crown – Violet/white

6. Brow/3rd Eye - Indigo

5. Throat - Blue

4. Heart - Green/pink

3. Solar Plexus - Yellow

2. Sacral - Orange

1. Base/Root - Red

Image 1 - Chakra zones of the body

My Conscious, Healing Moments

Section 1

Chapter 1 - Astral Healing

(Approximate age 5 – 8, years 1973-1976)

Like many other nights throughout my youth from when I was a very young child, all my dreams appeared to start off the same:

Always clothed in a pale pink silk robe, I rise out of my bed and float through my bedroom window. With a breaststroke action I float outside and fly around our big tree above our circular driveway. I 'swim' down the road, swimming faster and faster, floating higher and higher, feeling lighter and lighter. Rising above the trees in our suburb, the houses becoming smaller and smaller, finally vanishing as I rise higher, light and free in the warm night air. Brightly-lit stars become my guiding streetlights. The higher I go, the easier it is to fly, and I leave behind my swimming action.

This night I visit my dad in the Rhodesian Army. The location of the place is unknown to me. I see him seated and cleaning his rifle, with many other weapons lying around him. I float past, but he is unaware of my presence. I gently and teasingly tap one shoulder, while whispering "Hello Daddy" in his opposite ear. I fly through the roof and out into the bush. I am not afraid of this darkness and feel safe as there are others flying with me. I am not alone. One of the men flying with me reaches out his hand and leads me to thick, dense bush. We land gently, bare feet connecting firmly with the ground, unharmed by the thorny bushes and prickly, uncut grass. We bend over a man who is clutching his tummy from whence a river of blood is spilling onto the ground. Although the man is praying and crying out for help, his body is almost motionless. He catches a glimpse of us and asks who we are. My guiding man, who is holding my hand, gently places my one hand and his own on this man's tummy. I feel the warm blood as my hand rests on him. The wounded man is motionless. Then I see him rising out of his body and instinctively know that he is going to fly with us. We take off once more and as we rise, this injured man flies much higher than we do and then vanishes from sight. I hover over a tent hospital in the middle of the bush and then enter effortlessly right through the roof. With my guide still holding my hand, I land beside a stretcher on which an unconscious man is lying. His leg is broken at the knee. A shattered bone protrudes from the mashed flesh; blood oozes into the brown blanket. My guiding man gently places his hands on this man's leg. He does not wake up. I put my hand on him too. We stand this way for a short while and then fly away again- very, very fast this time. I instantly fly through my bedroom window and the next moment, find myself playing with my dolls. Feeling suddenly tired, I leap from one end of my room to the other, landing perfectly in bed, and the next moment I am fast asleep.

Self-Interpretation Of Astral Healing

As a child, I frequently woke up to find my dolls and toys on my bed, not in my cupboard where I had left them. I could never figure out how they got there at night. Apparently there were many times I would sleep-walk and play, seemingly without fear of roaming around outside in the dark. Unbeknown to me, I was always guided gently back to bed by my parents. This was far removed from the timid child I was in my waking hours—often filled with fear of the dark.

I regularly wondered why I was not able to fly in the daytime, the way I could at night when I was sound asleep.

In my dreams I always clothed myself in pink silk-pink being a spiritual colour of love. It brought with it a feeling of freedom and lightness, represented by floating. Using breaststroke was my most natural form of flight in my dream-state, recalling the swimming style I was good at in my real life.

The flying was also a past-life memory, from Atlantis times. I visited my dad in the army when I was feeling lonely and abandoned by him, this sense of abandonment connecting to a past-life experience. My spirit guides reminded me of my healing abilities. I believe now that I was actually healing others on the astral plane during this dream.

Chapter 2 - Connecting

(Approximate age 10, year 1978)

As a junior, I stayed at a hostel after school for day-care. My favourite game floats back to the windscreen of my mind: my friend, Pam, stands with eyes closed. I stand behind her, tapping her back in line with her heart. I slowly tie an invisible piece of string to Pam's back, make a knot and then pull this string towards me and up into the air. Using two hands, I slowly and gently pull the string until Pam starts falling backward. "Catch her quick!" everyone shouts. We love this game and always play it. On this particular day I stand with Pam, playing our game. I start pulling the string from her back, but this time, instead of pulling the string up, I pull it towards my body. I find myself shaking my head and blinking my eyes. It feels as if I am dreaming. I see a bolt of lightning flash from her back, across the invisible string, and right into my chest. I feel myself swaying. I notice we are swaying together, connected in rhythm. I feel myself falling. She is falling too. I can't stop and I panic. Then someone from behind catches me before I hit the ground.

We straighten up together, steadying ourselves and feeling very strange. "Wow, that was different!" we find ourselves exclaiming the same words at the same time. We laugh nervously. I turn around to see which of our other friends had caught me. There is nobody there! We are alone! The school field is deserted!

Pam and I look at each other. Something feels different and we look deep into each other's eyes. I am intensely aware of how close we feel. We go on with our lives in the days that follow and find ourselves avoiding our favourite game. As our friendship becomes even closer, we are amazed at how we keep saying the same things at the same time and even thinking the same things at the same time. We laugh even more. We even try to phone each other at the same time. We spend school holidays at one another's homes.

One day, Pam's mom takes us and her two younger sisters, Wendy and Kim, to town. It is hot and while Pam and her mom run quickly into a shop, I stay behind in the car to look after Wendy and Kim. We sit in silence, listening to the heat penetrating the metal of the car and the dashboard creaking with expansion. From the back seat I lean forward and look through the windscreen at the bonnet of the car. I see the heat waves gently rising off the car like small flames of invisible light. The heat is also rising from the road and pavement. People strolling past are oblivious to the rising flames they are stepping through. Sweat trickles down our bodies, a slow stream of salty body fluid.

Wendy and Kim become agitated as time begins to drag on. I try to amuse them by playing the little game of I-spy-with-my-little-eye. They are really very good at this and all too quickly guess my pictured words. Before long they are bored once more.

Kim attempts to escape out of the car in search of her mom.
"No," I shout, "you will get lost in the shop."

In desperation I find myself saying anything that comes to mind to keep her in the car.

"Your mom is coming now, I promise you," I say quickly with all the conviction I can muster.

"How do you know?" Wendy asks.

"I just know," I say hopefully, raising my finger to my mouth and saying "shh" so that her younger sister won't know I am lying, just to keep her in the car.

We sit silently for a few moments looking at the shop door in front of us. Within seconds, Pam and her mom come out. I sigh with genuine relief.

Later that afternoon Pam and I are swimming in their pool. She relates the earlier event in the shop with her mom and tells me, "We were standing in the shop with the cool fans blowing on us and I was thinking of how hot you all must be in the car. We had already made our purchase and my mom was browsing at the make-up section. I suddenly felt uncomfortable and told my mom we must go because it is very hot in the car."

We sit comparing our own separate, yet connected, events. We feel delighted in the knowledge that our thoughts are always aligned, even when we are not together. We often wonder if this is the way aliens speak to one another and project ourselves into the characters of the many storybooks we have read.

Although we are separated by fate at the end of our junior school years to attend different high schools, we vow to remain friends. (Our friendship never died.) We miss each other in our new schools, only visiting occasionally on weekends and holidays.

I find it impossible to form the same close friendship with anyone else in my new school. Two years later I am thrilled to be told I can attend the same school as my best friend. I even happen to be placed in the same class as Pam. Glorious!

Self-Interpretation Of Connecting

I created my own, conscious, energy connection to my friend in the string game. This is the same automatic cord connection we all energetically create when we connect and are in a relationship with one another. This connection strengthens the communication bond, via mental telepathy and all other levels too. This was the reason my friend and I were so in tune with one another, with thoughts and gestures.

One of my spirit guides must have been that 'being' that prevented me from falling that day. However, I never saw this being.

I was already immersed in human programming, or forgetfulness, in believing that a human was the only being around that could possibly have caught me.

My psychic vision was still open to seeing high vibrations of energy-as most children do. This was why I could see the heat rising off the car and paving while adults remained oblivious to this energy.

My friend's sisters were also still in touch with their natural born psychic abilities and could easily read my mind in the I-spy game, by using mental telepathy. The strong connection my friend and I had created gave us this deeper and instant ability to communicate via telepathy. This was why she

25

immediately knew of my dilemma of keeping her sisters in the car, and the reason for the escape attempt being the unbearable heat. She picked up my thoughts when I said their mom was coming and prompted their departure from the shop.

Chapter 3 - Premonitions

(Approximate age 14, year 1982)

My high school is on the opposite end of town to where I live. My mom drives me to Pam's house every morning and we cycle to school together from there. Then I spend my afternoons with her, until my mom collects me in the evening after work.

Today at school Pam learns she needs to stay at school for an after-school activity. I leave and ride to her house alone, wrapped up in my own thoughts that are running wild in my head. I know that Wendy and Kim will be wondering where she is when I arrive and I suddenly have this urge to play a joke on her sisters and to have some fun. I decide to tell them that she became ill at school today and was rushed to hospital and had to have an emergency appendix operation.

I laugh silently to myself, thinking this is really a cool joke to play on them. I wrestle for a moment with mixed feelings because I also feel sorry for her sisters and wonder how they are going to take the news. Although I know it's a joke, they don't. I ease my accusing conscience by thinking to myself that I will tell them the truth straight afterwards. I won't keep this joke going for too long. I feel satisfied with my decision and can't wait to see their faces.

When I finally arrive at their home, I have this uneasy feeling in my tummy. Opening the tall, black, patterned gate, I wonder for a moment whether I should rather forget about the joke.

Wendy and Kim run out eagerly to meet us and I see the surprise on their faces when they see that Pam is not with me. They immediately want to know where she is.

Here is my chance for a good prank, I decide, and ignoring the twinge of warning conscience, I decide to go for it and have some fun. I give them my rehearsed speech with so much feigned empathy that I even find myself moved to tears as I talk.

"I'm so sorry, but Pam was walking down the corridor today when she suddenly got such terrible pains in her tummy. She was bent over and unable to move and began to cry with pain. I ran to call the teacher and when we got back to her she had collapsed on the floor. The teacher and I dragged her to the first aid room and then called the ambulance. Pam was taken off to hospital to have her appendix removed."

Tears spring into their little eyes as the shocking news hits them like a ton of bricks. Not wanting to believe this terrible news, Wendy and Kim immediately voice their rejection with their synchronised "No-way, she must have stayed at school for something."

I stand my bike against the garage wall and follow them through the front door, ignoring Sam, their talking parrot, screeching "Hello Tina, Hello Tina".

I place my heavy schoolbag beside the table in preparation for homework. Thinking of how I can further convince them, I take on my most forlorn appearance: "The teacher called your mom and she went straight over to the hospital, I promise." The words "I promise" seem to penetrate, convincing them that my story must be true.

Wendy promptly announces, "I will call dad to take us to the hospital to see her."

In sudden panic I rush towards the phone to stop her. "No, Wendy," I yell, "I was only joking. Pam is at school, and she isn't in hospital."

Wendy and Kim are standing with confused and puzzled faces. It is clear that they don't know what to believe now. I spend the rest of the afternoon trying to convince them that I was only joking. I just hope they don't tell their mother about this nasty lie, I repeatedly think to myself.

As the long afternoon drags on, I am unable to focus on my homework. I go out of my way to play with Wendy and Kim to make sure they know it was only a joke. Finally all three of us laugh about the whole affair.

In the late afternoon my mom arrives to fetch me. Pam has still not arrived home and I again ignore this feeling of guilt and try to smother feelings of uneasiness. What on earth has happened to her?

I have a restless night, unable to stop thinking about Pam and the nasty prank I played on her sisters. What plagues my conscience is the recurring thought that I had blatantly lied to them.

The next morning when I arrive at Pam's home, feeling drowsy from an almost sleepless night, I am determined to push yesterday out of my mind and to conserve all my energy for the long day ahead.

Just as I close and latch the gate, Wendy runs out to meet me with the words, "Pam was admitted to hospital last night."

I turn to face her with chills running up and down my spine. A terrible feeling of déjà vu and an accusing "*what you sow is what you reap*" flash through my mind as I stare at the little girl.

I shake my head and try unsuccessfully to laugh while I explain to her that she can't play the same prank on me because it just won't work a second time. In a daze I feel the crisp morning air, far too chilling for this perfect, hot, summer's day, and it is somehow convincing me that my fears are about to be realised.

Wendy gasps for air and continues to explain as we walk side-by-side through the front door. Again my mind is too absorbed to make any attempt to greet Sam as he squawks my name in his parrot greeting. Wendy continues earnestly, "Pam arrived home shortly after you left here last night. She had taken a long time to ride home as she was in great pain. She had been feeling really sick all afternoon and the pain in her tummy was growing all the time. When she arrived home and climbed off her bike she bent over in terrible pain and was unable to move. She dropped her bike on the floor. I was running out to meet her and to tell her about your trick when I saw her crying and holding her tummy. Luckily mom had also just arrived home and I ran inside to call her. When we got back to Pam, she had collapsed. She was in dreadful pain. I told mom about the prank you played on us and she panicked. We all climbed into the car with mom and she rushed Pam to the hospital. The doctor said her appendix was about to burst and he had to do an emergency operation immediately to save her life."

My head is pounding. Everything feels so unreal, but the news is true! Sadness takes hold of me and an intense weariness engulfs every cell of my body. Their mom is at the hospital with Pam.

Their dad walks down the passage to greet me. "Can you please tell your teachers that Pam won't be at school for a couple of weeks," he asks.

"I will," I reply sheepishly and turn to leave. I have to leave for school now, or I will be late.

I climb on to my bike and leave. Without focusing on my surroundings I allow my subconscious mind to guide me over the familiar road I have travelled so many times before. I am feeling heavy and weak and alone, feeling bad, so bad, and so sad, hating and blaming myself. All the events of the preceding day are buzzing around wildly in my mind. How could I play such an awful prank on my friend's siblings? How could I ever have thought it was funny? What on earth made me do it? It was not fair. It was nothing short of heartless and I blame myself. Pam's condition is all my fault!

I simply cannot concentrate on anything at school. I ride home feeling terrible. I solemnly resolve to never again play a prank on anyone. I am such a bad person, I repeatedly tell myself, and I convince myself to never ever say or do anything like that again.

Self-Interpretation Of Premonitions

As a teen in high school, I was disconnecting even more from my psychic abilities and focusing on the 'external' and the 'physical' things around me, rather than the 'internal' gifts and abilities I was born with. I never understood how I could know something was about to happen. It isn't something taught in schools. How can it be? Our teachers, like most other adults, have totally forgotten these wonderful abilities within all of us. Our parents, now also in their adulthood, have normally forgotten too. At a young age, there appears to be no logical explanation for this phenomenon. When a child claims to see 'beings' (normally imaginary friends), parents correct them by telling them that their imagination is too fertile. Such parents are simply responding to their own frame of reference, according to what they 'think' they 'know' and understand. Children could be encouraged to trust their senses and be allowed to freely feel, experience and relate to the presence of these 'beings' who are, in fact, their own spirit guides or guardian angels.

Of course, my friends' sisters, at that early age, were not instantly going to believe me and 'instinctively' knew that I was lying. But notice how quickly I convinced them otherwise. It was wrong of me to make them doubt their wonderful God-given gift.

The whole episode turned out to be traumatic for me in the end. I did not understand it at that age. My friend's hospitalisation and our separation added to my anxiety. This experience inhibited me from seeking future friendships and close relationships. This then also kept me from sharing deeper truths with others. You can clearly discern which thoughts in that experience were my own and which were accurate premonitions. The event did not happen exactly as I said it would, due of course to the interference and creativity of my own mind and thoughts. For example, she did have appendicitis, but it happened at home and not at school as my fruitful mind related to the children.

Chapter 4 - Dreams Come True

(Approximate age 24, year 1992)

I had been having numerous problems relating to my womb. This particular morning I awake with a throbbing pain on the right side of my lower abdomen. My husband, leaves for work and I am left alone with our two small children, Casey and Dustin. I feel weak and the pain increases progressively. I consider going to the doctor but feel I had best not drive in my condition.

I get a phone call from my sister-in-law, Jane, and brother-in-law, Trevor, who tell me that they are going to the doctors' rooms and would like to visit afterwards. My immediate response is to ask if they could rather call around and pick me up to go with them to the doctors' rooms.

By the time we arrive, the minutes seem to be dragging ever so slowly as pain engulfs my body. I finally hobble in to see my doctor and painfully climb on to the examination bed. Tears of pain leap into my eyes when my doctor examines me. When he is through with his preliminary examination he admits me to hospital. He will visit later, after the required tests have been carried out to identify and pinpoint the exact problem. He suspects an ectopic pregnancy.

I return home, pack my bag and head straight for the hospital. The pain is almost unbearable. Trevor has to help me into a wheelchair and push me to the hospital bed that my doctor has booked for me. Trevor and Jane agree to take care of Casey and Dustin.

I am set up with an intravenous drip and undergo several tests. The sonar provides evidence of a cyst on the right ovary. I finally drift off to sleep and have the following disturbing dream.

My doctor is flying alone in his microlight and I am floating like an angel beside his airborne vehicle as I watch him fly. I am wondering why I don't need a microlight to fly as I watch him being kept aloft so effortlessly by the red and white craft. He approaches a mountain too quickly and crashes his microlight on top of the rocks. His body has been impaled by the smashed aircraft and jagged rocks. Blood seeps out of his shoe. I quickly float down to him and see that many angels have joined me. I reach out to him with the assurance that all will be well. He shakes his head in pain and in his weakening state he tells me that 'this is it", that he is dying and no-one knows where he is or that he had crashed. I assure him 'this is not the end' and he is not going to be leaving me again. Messages have been sent and will bring help in time.

In desperation I encourage him, words tumbling from my mouth. I watch as angels gather around him and place their hands on different areas of his body. We maintain eye contact as they silently speak directly in my mind.

"This is how you channel energy to another." It is as if I am in training. It feels like time is passing too slowly; he lies trapped for too long. His heart rate is flagging and with many internal injuries, pain engulfs him. Finally, a helicopter arrives to transport him to hospital. I stand aside, place my hand on his shoulder and send energy, as the angels had just taught me. I comfort him and say, "I will visit you in hospital". As he is lifted into the helicopter, I hear the machines that have just been attached beeping loudly. His heart has stopped and he is dying, I think to myself. That is why he has so many angels with him now. I float away alongside some of the angels with the instinctive knowledge that our work is done. I leave my doctor in the helicopter in the company of the two angels. Almost instantly I float down to re-enter my body, sleeping peacefully in a strange hospital bed.

I wake slowly from my dream, only to experience instant panic, disorientation and fear as I recall my doctor's accident. Relief floods through me when I realise I am in the hospital and it was just a dream. But my troubled mind tells me that the dream was too real, too chilling, and I am extremely concerned.

I ask if my doctor has been to visit me. He hasn't.

I try to wait patiently, but the dream replays clearly in my mind. My uneasiness is mounting. Time passes and he still doesn't arrive. It is late afternoon and I become impatient with the nurses and want them to call him. I am both angry and worried now and ask myself how he could admit me to this hospital bed and then not follow up. By this time medication has mercifully diminished my pain and I want to go home, to get away from this hospital which has become the scene for this troubling dream.

The nurses continue trying to get hold of him and it is only very late in the afternoon that they find out where he is. One of them informs me, "Your doctor is out flying his microlight. We have left a message with his wife for him to come to the hospital when he returns."

Fear grips my insides. I can't believe what they're telling me. This can't be true! Instead of the news calming me, I worry more and fear that he is not coming back at all. My dream was so real. And so the fear grows. I wonder whether another doctor can discharge me. All the while my anger is growing and I'm torturing myself for having such a stupid dream.

When he finally walks into the ward, hours later, I am so relieved. It was only a nightmare and he is blissfully unaware of my dream, my thoughts and my fears on his behalf. He is, mercifully, still alive and well. My fear and anger instantly get the better of me and like a leaping wolf I attack him as he approaches my bed. "How can you just admit a patient and then fail to follow up and discharge me?" I fling at him in hot anger, blurting the words from my own needs, anguish and concern for his wellbeing.

"I did follow up over the phone," he assures me after recovering from my verbal attack. "I knew you needed to rest so I took my weekly afternoon off, knowing you were in good hands."

His reply satisfies my tortured mind, as well as my need for further medication, but my dream was still just too real for my satisfaction.

The next morning he arrives to discharge me from hospital. I have regained a measure of sanity and peace and try hard to push the dream from my mind.

Months follow, with my dream constantly plaguing my memory and haunting me every time it flashes to mind. I can't eradicate it, no matter how hard I try. I replace the scenes of the dream with other thoughts each time they occur, but then find that something else invariably draws my attention back, almost as if they are making sure I don't forget.

I pick up magazines that have microlights in them. I see microlights on the TV. I hear someone on the radio talking about microlights. Every weekend, when I spend time outside absorbing the peace and fresh air, someone flies their microlight overhead.

I'm attending computer-college and during lunch break I happen to walk down the street and around the corner. There, right in front of me, large as life and squatting on a trailer is, guess what? Yes, right; another microlight. My dream thunders back into my troubled mind and my insides start churning all over again. I stare fixedly at the red sail and wonder why this is happening to me. Perhaps I need to see a psychologist, I tell myself, because I suspect that I am being driven crazy by a dream.

By now I am angry with myself for being weak enough to allow this dream to haunt me around every corner. Am I perhaps trying too hard to push it from my mind?

But that is not the end of it. I keep 'accidentally' bumping into my doctor in the most unexpected places. Each meeting reminds me afresh of my dream. I keep telling myself to be happy that he didn't crash his microlight, that he is alive and that it was only a dream. But who am I bluffing? I am only running from the recurring reminder of this dream.

One day I take my daughter to see the doctor and in the waiting room I pick up the first magazine I can reach. The back page has a microlight on it again. "Why won't this dream leave me?" I ask myself irritably. "I manage to forget many other dreams very quickly, so why should this one be so different?" Some of the folk in the room look at me quizzically, but I ignore them and continue paging idly through the magazine. I am unable to concentrate until I see a large caption that leaps out of the page at me. It says, "Tell Him". The article does not interest me, but the two words hold my attention with riveting power.

Immediately I am in deep debate with my thoughts. I can't tell my doctor about a silly dream? Sure I can. No, I can't. Why not? Because he'll laugh at me, that's why. He'll think I've lost it.

Days go by and the myriad signs continue indicating my need to tell him. I keep asking myself, over and over, whether I have the right to tell him, to warn him of something that might-or might never-happen. Perhaps I will just create fear in him, I tell myself in one moment. The next instant, I comfort myself with the thought that it was just a dream. This is the way he should hear it. I must tell him I had a dream about him. He can make up his own mind. The fact of the matter is that I have to talk about it to get it out of my mind and, hopefully, find peace in doing so.

I finally pluck up the courage to tell him. As I feared, my words come out all wrong; nothing like I had rehearsed in my mind. My fears take hold again and, in mid-sentence, I stop. I choose not to tell him. I leave without mentioning anything about him and his microlight. As I leave I feel the terrible hauntings of the dream once more and feel additional guilt mounting in my conscience.

Some weeks later when I arrive at the doctor's rooms to pay an account, the friendly dispensary lady asks me, "Have you heard what happened to your doctor?"

Immediately I feel myself go cold and start shivering, "No, I haven't," I reply in a small voice.

"He had an accident in his microlight and is now in hospital," she continues. "He was seriously injured and was in intensive care for some time. We didn't think he was going to make it."

I stare at her in horror as she continues. "Fortunately, he is recovering."

I'm shaking uncontrollably and without the need of a mirror I know that the blood has drained from my face. She sees my shock and places her comforting hand on my shoulder. "We were all very shocked at the news, just as you are."

Almost in a dream state, I cannot believe what I am hearing. I manage to sit down and compose myself and suddenly know and understand the need for the persistent reminders of my own dream. I feel terrible–as if I missed something very important.

Back in my car I sit motionless, the shocking news causing my body to shake uncontrollably. How could I have missed it? At the shop I buy a card and immediately head for the hospital. When I peep into his room he is asleep. I place the card on the bedside unit and leave silently without disturbing him. I still cannot understand how I managed to ignore the subtle, and the not-so-subtle, prompts, hints and urges to tell him.

After his full recovery I have the courage to discuss the accident with him, and I discover my graphic dream reflects his experience with astonishing similarities. I am still disappointed, even angry, with myself for knowing something was going to happen and not having the courage to speak up. I may have been able to caution him had I not allowed my fears to rule my decisions. However, it is a lesson well learned. It will stand me in good stead in my own life and personal development.

Self-Interpretation Of Dreams Come True

Without any of us realising it at the time, we were all communicating via mental telepathy, even before the telephone call from Jane and Trevor about the visit to the doctor.

The pain associated with my right ovary cysts began to indicate an underlying trauma deep within me.

I learned that the probable cause of ovary problems had to do with my creativity–the ovary representing the point of creativity. This was where my early childhood sexual abuse began to show. The sexual abuse I suffered robbed me of my sensual creativity at that tender age, also without my consent, and it suppressed my psychic abilities thereafter.

As it was presenting on the right side of my body, it reflected my perception of fatherhood, brotherhood and my view of men in general. This also reflected my pattern of habitually giving myself away in some manner to men; not letting go of the events caused by the sexual abuse-the 'masculine energy'.

The cyst signified that the memories of my childhood sexual abuse were continuing to play out, in a painful, continuous 'loop'. This presented as major hurt, which was, in turn, suppressed by anger. My body was, on its own, working through this trauma and releasing it on a subconscious level, while trying to get my attention through physical symptoms.

My dream was all the while reawakening my psychic abilities. Bear in mind that I had blocked off these abilities in early childhood, then reinforced the obstruction through the trauma when Pam had her appendix removed.

Separation anxiety resurfaced in hospital, as it had with my childhood friend. As I mentioned, it is interesting to note that this dream once again involved a male. See what mental torture I put myself through once more, clearly pointing to much suppressed trauma and anxiety. And that was now being compounded by this latest ordeal.

In the interpretation of dreams, flying can represent sexuality, while rocks can represent inner strength. The mountain on which the accident happened pointed to an obstacle ahead that needed to be overcome. Fortunately, the accident happened on the top of the mountain and not in the middle or at the bottom—the subconscious thereby informing that I was on top of the problem and would in fact get through it. My spiritual guides were clearly making their presence known by leading and teaching me healing techniques that I employ to this day.

Because of my own past problems, recalled by my creative mind, my doctor's accident was remarkably akin to my own mountain-and-rocks dreams.

Even at that stage my spirit guide communication was constant, without me being aware of it. They were prompting me, through my subconscious, to communicate with my doctor. But of course I did not know about, let alone acknowledge, spirit guides at that stage of my life. I simply believed I was crazy. Every time I told myself I needed to see a psychologist, I was actually awakening the psychologist deep within me, quite unaware of it at the time. I was also slowly awakening my own mental and emotional powers of healing and my psychic abilities.

Sadly, though, the trauma caused by the confusion of all these experiences buried my anxiety ever deeper and sent me into silent depression.

I was being guided to release the burden I had created for myself-my friend's hospital experience as a child, to this latest experience, by communicating with my doctor. It was just too difficult for me to find the correct words. Not going ahead and speaking, though, lead to my communications becoming more deeply suppressed.

Chapter 5 – Loving Hands

(Approximate age 27, year 1995)

I am about to undergo a partial hysterectomy by laser surgery to remove my diseased uterus. I lie in the cold theatre room, anxiously awaiting my turn. There is an uneasy feeling deep within me today, an inexplicable fear lurking in the deep recesses of my mind. I slowly become aware of a strange, yet comforting and warm, sensation settling close to my right shoulder. While it feels as if someone is standing beside me, I see only nurses and doctors, who are all busy, across the room. I feel a light, warm pressure on my skin and I imagine that someone is holding my hand. I feel comforted and peaceful. A serene, calming peace spreads over my entire body. I hear words mulling through my mind as if someone is talking to me.

"*I am close to you. You are protected and safe. Don't fight the coming events–go with them and enjoy. Focus on breathing.*"

The theatre nurse appears and wheels me into theatre. Before long, my doctor enters and takes my hand to begin the general anaesthetic. I begin trembling because I fear something is just not right. I have had many anaesthetics before, but there is a very different and ominous feeling about this one. He calms me down and tells me not to worry because it will soon be over. I can't bear this unsettled feeling. When he asks me to breathe and relax, I wonder if he knows how I am shaking deep within.

My gynaecologist, on my left, moves closer and asks if I am ready to begin. Although I nod 'yes', deep inside I am actually saying 'no'. I turn back to my doctor. The look in his eye frightens me; I feel he is scrutinising my deepest fears. When the prick of the needle comes I inhale sharply in fear and shake my head, trying to say 'no'. I gasp for air and hear my doctor repeating, "breathe deeply, breathe deeply". "Too late," I think. "I don't have enough air and I can't breathe." Then, mercifully, the anaesthetic kicks in and blanks my mind.

I wake up in recovery with severe aching in my abdomen. There are distant voices in the room and although someone is holding my hand, I am crying because of the pain. The voice of the recovery nurse is somewhat comforting, but I continue to squirm in pain.

I drift fitfully in and out of sleep, still fully aware of the persistent pain and when I awake, startled, in the intensive care unit, there is the sound of equipment beeping behind me. The squirming immediately starts again and I tearfully fight against the pain. My doctor is sitting near my bed and I immediately notice that there is a strange silence about him. He stands up, moves to my bedside and reaches for my hand. "I need something for pain," I tell him even before he can speak.

"I can't give you anything right now," he replies. "Your blood pressure is very low."

I feel my body tensing as the pain increases with each twinge. It's a hot, burning, intense pain, deep inside my womb. "I can't take this pain. It is too sore," I cry out.

He squeezes my hand in a comforting gesture. "I'm sorry, I can't give you anything right now. Just try to relax".

I think to myself, *how can I possibly relax with such intense pain*?

He leaves after telling me that he will be back again later to see how I'm doing.

I'm left alone with the sounds of beeping all around me. I feel the blood pressure machine squeezing my arm painfully every 15 minutes or so as I drift in and out of sleep.

My husband comes to visit that evening and attempts to cheer me with his great sense of humour. He tells me I look like Robocop with so many wires and machines attached to my body. All I do is complain about the pain and grumble about not being given anything to alleviate it.

How ridiculous! How can anyone be expected to recover from an operation without any painkillers? I am angry and hungry, yet very alert. My mind is now completely clear and I am conscious of everything around me. Yes, to make matters worse, I am not allowed to eat either. The nurse explains that it is a precaution in case I need to go back to theatre. When I ask why, she explains that my blood pressure is dangerously low. She reinforces my need to relax my body.

I am left feeling alone once more. I look across the room and see the woman who went into theatre for her hysterectomy just before me. She is sitting up, eating, and when she has had her fill, she gets out of bed and walks around. I find it very strange and unfair. I ask my nurse, "Why is that lady able to eat and walk around?"

The nurse explains that her blood pressure is normal, she is on painkillers and that she has very little pain right now. I am envious and jealous of her as I continue to fight the intense pain that constantly consumes my body in vicious waves. I find it impossible to relax and am so annoyed that people expect me to relax in this situation. How would they feel if they were to recover without painkillers? Each time the nurses check the machines attached to me, I ask if my blood pressure is normal enough for painkillers. Every time the reply is the dreaded 'no'.

I finally decide that I've had enough of this pain. Desperation is mounting and I start praying in real anger for God's help. "God, I can't take any more of this. I just can't handle this pain. Please take it away now! Or let me die-I am ready to die now. I just can't live through this pain."

I keep repeating this prayer, and when it becomes apparent that nothing is changing, I ask Him if he can indeed hear me. I am really mad now and express my anger out-loud.

Suddenly my machines are beeping wildly. The nurses rush over to me, demanding that I calm down. "Your blood pressure is out of control, lady," one of them shouts to me. "Call the doctor immediately!" I hear the nurse shout in fear. "Breathe deeply and relax," she tells me.

"I can't. I need painkillers," I say.

"I can't do it," the nurse says. "You can't have painkillers because they will kill you right now!"

I feel her anger and fears beamed at me and hear her harsh words hitting home like a hammer. Just what I needed to hear and just what I wanted to happen!

Suddenly the thought crosses my mind that maybe I am really dying. The next moment my mind is off at another tangent and I desperately force myself to breathe with the pain, trying to get a grip on myself and to do what is good for me. I simply have to force myself to relax. One nurse stays with me this time, repeatedly telling me to relax and to breathe.

On my doctor's entry, I immediately sense the urgency, the fear and compassion rolled into one. He also sternly advises me to relax and in the same breath apologises for not being able to give me something for the pain. He squeezes my knee and walks away, in conversation with the nurse. I'm left alone and praying once again. "God, I can't do this alone, I just can't." The pain continues.

Sometime later, another doctor appears beside me. He is Japanese, wears a typical white coat and has a stethoscope around his neck. He places his hand on top of mine and immediately an amazing sense of peace descends over me. "Tina," he says, with the same sternness as my own doctor, "You unfortunately have to get through this without painkillers, but you are not alone."

I immediately start protesting but stop in mid-sentence when he lifts my hand. "I am here to show you how to get through this," he says gently, and places both my hands, one over the other, on my painful womb. Then he very gently rests his hands on top of mine. His touch is ever so light. He encourages me to breathe in deeply, long and slow, with every wave of pain. "Don't remove your hands at all," he says. "Focus on the pain subsiding as you breathe out very, very slowly. Imagine you are slowly blowing at a candle without letting the flame go out. Imagine a white, warming light covering your hands, penetrating your body. Feel the warmth deep within you. Send loving thoughts into your hands and through them direct the energy towards your insides. Don't allow your focus to shift. Go beyond the pain. Rise above it. By keeping your eyes closed you will be able to keep focused. Know and remember that you are not alone. Help is close at hand."

I try this out as he is talking. I become aware of just how calm and peaceful I am. I hear a man coughing and choking in a bed nearby. The doctor and I both look in his direction. The doctor immediately excuses himself. "I have to leave now," he says over his shoulder. "But remember that you are not alone." With that, he walks over to attend to the coughing man.

Pain immediately engulfs my thoughts again as I watch him depart, but then I focus on what this unusual doctor has just taught me. I do as he told me. I remember the same candle during my labour at the birth of my first child, my daughter, Casey. I recall with a little surprise that I have done this before. I got through that intense pain by focusing on my breathing, with this same candle. How strange. My thoughts drift back over the years and I think about how significant it is that this doctor should speak about the candle and procedures I have seen and followed before. Strange, too, how soon, and how easily, one forgets.

I think about how comfortable and peaceful I felt while this doctor was with me. What a weird feeling! I continue focusing on helping myself by doing everything, just as I was taught.

I hear the blood pressure machine beeping and tell myself that I have a goal to accomplish here. The first step is to normalise my blood pressure. I consciously focus on my blood flowing through my arteries and on my heart beating. I imagine increasing my strength with each heartbeat. I visualise the nurse checking my blood pressure. When she comes, I think of myself asking her how I am doing.

She is shocked. There is finally a great and inexplicable improvement. While it is much better, it is still not quite normal yet. I am greatly encouraged and continue this focusing process. I feel strength within me and have a feeling of peace and wellbeing. I am not alone! I start thanking God for sending me another doctor to help me deal with the pain and for reminding me to use some of the techniques I already knew, as well as some new ones. What a blessing!

Comfortable contentment is slowly growing in me. I am awake all night, focusing on what needs to be done to help myself. I finally ask the nurse who the doctor was who visited me earlier, as he didn't give me his name. I tell her that I really want to thank him for his help. The nurse looks at me strangely and then utters the words that send chills up my spine. "Doctor? What doctor? No doctor visited you, my dear." She checks the record chart, checks with the other nurses and then tells me that, definitely, no doctor had visited me since my doctor had done so. She explains that as I was in extreme pain I had probably dreamt the whole thing. I, however, know that it was real. I know that my eyes were open all the time and that I felt his hands on mine. I know that I heard all his words and that I was definitely not dreaming this time. His presence was real and I know he was there, whether in the flesh or otherwise. Being Japanese and wearing a white coat, I admit, is rather unusual, in a South African hospital. Was he not perhaps a spirit guide? I ask myself. I'm not quite ready to accept this latest thought. Before long, however, I find myself tempted to believe what the nurse is telling me. Was it, then, my imagination, or was it real? I ask the nurse how the man who was coughing and choking is doing. I point towards the bed nearby, the man the nameless doctor went to attend to.

"He passed away rather suddenly" she tells me. "He died of pneumonia. He was very old."

I feel quite creepy, realising that a man died so close to me while I was completely unaware of it. I again focus on my present circumstances and try to forget the incident.

Early morning arrives with the discovery that my blood pressure is normal. A remarkable goal has been achieved. When the nurse tells me that I am now allowed to have some painkillers, I laugh and tell her that I no longer need them as I have very little pain. Now it is her turn to be surprised. What a change in attitude, she must have thought.

My doctor visits and he is also amazed at my improvement. I have my usual smile again. Now that I am stronger he tells me what happened. "Your heart stopped during the operation, which is why you are so weak and were unable to have pain medication." I ask if I am allowed to have the catheter removed so I can go to the toilet. At first he's a little hesitant and asks, "Are you sure you're really ready to get up and walk?"

"Yes, I am," I reply.

"Okay," he concedes, "But you will need to be very careful because you're going to feel faint-and only after you have eaten something. The nurse has to be with you, too."

I know this will be quite an achievement. I am in the corner bed in the intensive care unit, on the far side from the door that leads to the bathrooms. I feel inspired every time I see the woman who had also had a hysterectomy walking about.

Now, with most of the wires and tubes disconnected, I am finally up and out of bed. With only a drip still connected, a rush of dizziness overtakes me and I feel as if I am going to faint. The nurse sits me down on a chair and gets me to relax, breathing deeply and slowly. I get to my feet again, taking one small step at a time. Painful muscle spasms cause me to stop after almost every other step. Then I breathe, focus, and relax, placing my hands on my tummy while recalling the past night's events. I find the going very tough, but reject every thought of returning to that bed in defeat. My goal is to reach that toilet and in my mind's eye I see the other lady and I push on, knowing that if she can do it, then I can too. How much further can it be? Eventually the marathon is over and I arrive at my destination. I go in alone, relaxing, breathing and focusing through the pain. While the nurse waits for me on the other side of the door, I congratulate myself for having walked so far with so much pain in every step. Once finished, the painful journey back to bed awaits. I am extremely weak, out of breath and dizzy again. I wish for wings to simply fly back to bed, but remember who and what I am as I take the first painful step of the second marathon that day. Plodding painfully, one step at a time, I finally reach the soft haven and crawl back into the soft, comforting bed. When my head hits the pillow I immediately drift off into a peaceful sleep for the first time since being in theatre the day before.

With the rejuvenation of sleep, I am well on the road to a speedy recovery. I awake with renewed strength and motivation. Pleased, yet envious, I greet my lady friend who is being discharged. I realise I now have a new goal, small as it may be: going home. Now I use the trips to the toilet as a gauge for my recovery, each visit adding to my speed and stamina. I'm walking alone and learn from the nurses that one visits the toilet more frequently after the removal of a catheter. They are not aware that my frequent visits to the ladies' rooms are actually driven by my burning desire to go home. I constantly encourage myself by remembering the words of the nameless doctor, "You are not alone."

Now I am finally beginning to understand what this really means. I find myself accepting the thought of having spirit guides around me all the time.

It is morning and my doctor orders my release from intensive care to a ward, to complete my recovery and regain my strength. When he visits again in the late afternoon, I am now far stronger, full of the joys of life and I have very little pain. I am sitting on the bed eating dried fruit, watching the sun's rays filtering through the window. My doctor is pleased with my progress and discharges me.

Home sweet home, in the familiar surroundings of my own making, I recover rapidly, often reviewing the healing journey. With a sense of pride, I reflect on the unusual feat of recovering from a partial hysterectomy without painkillers.

Self-Interpretation Of Loving Hands

In applying the concept of metaphysical causation, I realise the cause of the need for a hysterectomy was due to the suppressed trauma of sexual abuse. This energy, which I had not confronted, connected too many suppressed thoughts and emotions still present. These had been building up over decades. I had growths on the outside of the uterus.

Over the years I had stored up resentment towards my sexual abuser, and this caused many problems in adulthood. So many traumas had become deeply embedded within me.

My own fear of trusting and believing disappeared the moment I started sensing the presence of my guides again. I was shifting out of denial and progressing in awareness. I felt my guide touching me.

This most painful experience was necessary to awaken me to healing. It was a wonderful opportunity, and gift, to practice doing without the help of medicine. My spirit guide ensured that I saw, felt and heard him all the time. My spirit guide had been with me at the birth of my daughter, had shown me the candle as a way of controlling my breathing through pain; and reminded me, here again. Notice how I positively created a healing goal and then set out to achieve it. My positive attitude and confidence in healing has now become more obvious, of course, bringing much gratitude for an experience through illness.

Chapter 6 - Healing Visitors

(Approximate age 29, year 1997)

After a really difficult morning at work, feeling weak with diarrhoea and nausea, I decide to go home and rest. Driving home, the nausea rises fast and furious with the motion of the car. I tell myself not to vomit. Arriving home, I climb weakly from the car-and vomit before I reach the gate. My head pounding, stars floating before my eyes, I hang onto the gate for support. I finally get the gates open, bring my car in and make my way into the house. In the kitchen I pour a glass of water, but have to put it aside quickly as the intense nausea again forces me to vomit–this time into the sink. I clean up and take my glass of water to the bedroom with me. Sitting on the side of the bed, I kick off my shoes and take a small, slow sip of water. I reach across to my nightstand for some pain tablets for my pounding head, only to discover the bottle is empty.

Too weak to move, I pull the duvet over my legs and lie still. Breathing deeply and relaxing consciously with my eyes closed, I place my hands on my stomach. I am determined not to vomit again. This is where I drift off into dreamland.

I am dreaming that I am sick and resting on my bed. I hear an old couple talking at the front door. I am too weak to go to the door to see who they are. From what they say, I gather they are here to help me. Fear grips me when I wonder how they managed to come through the closed door.

I am astounded to see my great-grandfather and great-grandmother walking through my bedroom doorway to stand beside my bed. I recognise them from my very early childhood. They both died when I was young. I tell myself that it is impossible for them to be here–after all, they're dead.

I am feeling too weak to move or even to talk to them, but watch them with wide eyes.

My great-grandfather kneels beside my bed, his warm, tender and very light hand comforting mine. My hands are in the same position as they were in when I went to sleep. My great-grandmother gently sits down in the middle of my bed. She leans on her elbow and runs her fingers through my hair.

I tell myself I am dreaming and force myself to wake up.

I am desperately trying to wake up and can hear the dogs barking wildly outside. For the life of me, I am unable to open my eyes. While I try to force them open, I feel a weight lifting from the bed, beside my legs. When I finally manage to force my eyelids apart, I sit up with my heart pounding in my chest. I feel rather shaken at having been consciously aware of someone on my bed, yet unable able to see anyone in the room now. I tell myself I am just weak and delirious and that it was only a dream. The very real presence lifting off the bed while I was completely aware of the dogs barking and the strange way in which my eyes wouldn't open, is just too bizarre to laugh off.

I reach for my glass of water and slowly sip the last dregs, too afraid to actually move off the bed.

I hear voices again, coming from the front door. I shake my head repeatedly, telling myself that I am having a nutty moment. I pick up my book from my nightstand to distract my thoughts and find, after a few moments, that I am reading words that aren't making any sense as I am totally unable to focus. On the positive side, I am aware that I am feeling much better. My nausea and vomiting have ceased and the headache is almost gone. I remain on the bed all day, waiting for my husband to come home.

Self-Interpretation Of Healing Visitors

Clearly an event at work that morning triggered my sense of fear and rejection and brought on the diarrhoea, nausea and vomiting.

Perhaps this was the first phase in my being directed towards accepting that change of career was on its way. Was being shown that I was to work from home? Up to that point I had rejected the notion, hence in accordance with metaphysical causation the vomiting. Once again, not having medication available, I was forced to take on natural healing techniques. Quite frankly, I was not aware of what I was doing at the time. Notice that in my unawareness, I was guided to place my hands on my abdomen. This was far more deliberate and precisely guided than I realised at the time.

I realised, too, that this was fast becoming a natural action for me. I experienced this lucid dream because my guides were bringing my healing abilities to my attention. (A lucid dream is where you are aware that you are dreaming while you are, in fact, still asleep.)

At this time my own energy vibration had changed, which is what was required for me to see and/or feel my spirit guides. Guides have a much lighter vibration than we do in our dense, human bodies, and we are usually unable to sense them. Of course, now in adulthood myself, I had long forgotten the vibration to connect to them. However, they were ensuring I remembered this feeling, through the lucid dream-state. They were reawakening me. And I was aware of the healing that came from this. I learned, too, that our spirit guides truly guide, support and heal us even when we are unaware of their presence and, regardless of any gratitude to them. I think we can be quite disrespectful to their presence in our lack of awareness.

I also continued rationalising, to convince myself that spirit guides did not exist. Certainly a tug of war and change in my belief structure was taking place! The fear that arose in me after the dream indicated that my senses were well aware of their spiritual presence. I was learning to accept this as definitely not to be written off as 'craziness'.

Chapter 7 - Knowing

(Approximate age 30, year 1998)

My very close aunt, who I always felt was more like a second mother to me, is arriving with my uncle from Zimbabwe to visit us in South Africa. They are staying with us on Mother's Day. I search high and low to find the perfect Mother's Day gift for her and finally find a beautiful brooch, with two doves in flight. Just perfect, I think.

Mother's Day arrives and my aunt is pleased with her gift. She has recovered from a mastectomy from breast cancer and, more recently, a heart attack. This trip to South Africa is partly for a check-up with one of our specialists.

We take her to our local Bokkie Park, a petting zoo, to visit the animals. She has a special interest in farm animals, having assisted my uncle on his farm.

She enjoys the outing but before long complains of heartburn. A little concerned, we decide to go home to allow her to rest. She insists I take a look at the scar from the removal of her breast. Feeling most uncomfortable, I agree to see it. I find myself more troubled over what the reason could be for her wanting to show it to me than her insistence that I see the huge scar across her chest. Unable to figure out her reasoning, I choose to forget about it. Strangely, though, there is a close, inexplicable connection between us, as if some silent communication is taking place.

The day comes to an end and my aunt and uncle are departing to spend a week with her sister. We say our good-byes for the time being and I stand in the driveway, waving as the car moves away. I suddenly have a strong premonition that I am not going to see my aunt again. She turns around in the car and waves. This strong awareness is telling me that this is good-bye forever. At that moment a bee buzzes around my head and the thought crosses my mind that every time a bee buzzes near me in the future I will know that she is present. The doves of her Mother's Day gift leave me with a similar feeling. I dispel these seemingly silly thoughts and move on with my life.

It's a Tuesday evening when we receive the call: my aunt has had another heart attack and is in hospital. I decide not to go to the hospital because I know we have already said good-bye. I know I have made the right decision when my parents find that they are too late when they arrive at the hospital. She has already passed away.

At her funeral I am given back the brooch I had given her just days earlier. I am most upset that this brooch is not being buried with her, but I take it and leave it on top of my dressing table. I so wished it could have been with her in her grave.

Two days later the brooch goes missing from my dressing table, never to be found again.

Self-Interpretation Of Knowing

My healing intuition is now greatly developed. I sensed my aunt's heart problems. I also picked up on the mental telepathy that took place between us; two Souls communicating. Both of us knew, from deep within, what was ahead.

Chapter 8 - Hazy Hand

(Approximate age 30, year 1998)

I'm experiencing painful, tender breasts that are both hard and sore. I go to my doctor to find out what is wrong. I am given medication and I am also sent for a mammogram. The latter reveals that while there is dense fibro-adenosis present, there are, mercifully, no cysts or lumps.

A month later I'm back with my doctor, still with discomfort and no improvement from the prescribed medication. He sends me to a specialist for a procedure that involves drawing off surrounding fluid for testing.

I am feeling extremely uncomfortable as I enter the waiting room. I try to convince myself that I am only fearful because I am seeing a new doctor. When I enter the doctor's room I'm shocked by his rather abrupt and rude introduction. He sits down in his chair without speaking so I make myself comfortable in a chair opposite him, without an invitation, and place my mammogram and referral letter on his desk.

I bring him up to speed about what has taken place to date and that my doctor would like him to do the tests. I also tell him that my doctor said he could call him while I was there if there was anything else he would like to know. In an abrupt, raised voice he tells me that *no* other doctor *ever* tells *him* what to do. Visibly annoyed, he goes on to say that the only reason for my tender and sore breasts is that, like all women, I'm undergoing hormonal changes in my breasts from menstruation–don't I know that?

My own anger starts to mount now, triggered by his disrespectful tone. He hasn't bothered to call my doctor or to ask for any input from me. After all, I'm only the patient here! How ignorant does he think I am? He arrogantly assumes that because I am young, the only cause can be menstruation.

This is where I raise my voice to him. "I don't have periods, Doctor. For your information, I have had a hysterectomy."

He is visibly shocked. "What did you have that for?" he asks when he recovers his composure and his arrogant bearing. "You are young. Have you even had children yet?"

I hold his gaze unflinchingly while I wonder what his precise problem is. Does he speak to all his patients like this, or is there just something he doesn't like about *me*?

He lowers his gaze to read the details on my form, almost as if he is trying to escape my angry glare. "Yes, I have two children. My family is complete," I answer angrily, ignoring the first part of his question.

He looks at me differently now, aware too of the mutual, silent animosity between us. "Well then," he breaks the silence, "let's take a look. Go into that room". He points to the door behind me. "Take everything off and put on the gown".

"Everything?" I ask in alarm, wondering why I should strip down completely when I am here to have my breasts checked.

"That's right. You heard me correctly," he says with smug satisfaction without looking my way.

Inside the room I remove only the top half of my clothing and then put the gown on too.

He enters and pulls the gown open and proceeds to prod my breasts with rough, insensitive hands. I wonder if this man actually heard me telling him my breasts are sore. Perhaps he just doesn't care.

"It is quite dense," he admits. "Get dressed and come through."

I dress quickly and take a seat opposite him again. He ignores me for some time while he takes a personal telephone call and chats away casually as if I were not present. When he finally ends the call he announces, "The best thing for us to do then is not to waste time testing the breast, but rather to remove all the dense tissue immediately".

"Remove *all* the dense tissue?" I gasp in total horror, knowing full well that it would involve most of my breast tissue.

"Yes," he replies dogmatically, in a tone aimed at squashing all argument.

By now I have taken more from this rude man than I can stomach. I stand up, reach across the desk and grab my mammogram with blazing eyes. "Thanks, but no thanks," I hiss into his startled face. "That will mean that I'll have no breasts *left* when you're through with your one-track procedure!"

I storm out of his rooms angrier than I have ever been. Fully enraged and not willing to hide it, I climb into the car where my husband has been patiently waiting for me. He sees the thunder clouds around my head and asks what happened. I am too angry to talk for the moment. Shaking my head in shock, I burst into tears. I tell him what happened and ask him to take me straight back to my doctor.

In the waiting room I am too mad to think about appointment procedures and sit waiting until he is free. Anger, disappointment and shock still rage in me.

I finally sit before my doctor and tell him about the catastrophic appointment. I want his verdict since I have now lost all confidence in specialists and tell him as much. I insist that *he* draw the fluid for the tests.

"I can't," he explains. "Only a specialist is qualified to carry out that procedure."

I inform him that I couldn't care less whether he is qualified or not. I know how much I trust him to do it correctly. He goes ahead and arranges for me to be at the hospital in the morning for the procedure, under local anaesthetic.

I arrive on the morrow, visibly much calmer than the day before and ready to go through with it. My doctor enters the theatre waiting room and asks how I am and whether I am calmer than yesterday. I am now feeling embarrassed about the previous day. I had no right to vent my anger at him.

"Yes, I'm calm thanks," I assure him and blush with the admission.

He outlines the procedure and informs me that he has arranged for a new specialist to carry it out. While he is not permitted to perform the procedure, he assures me that he will be present as the anaesthetist.

I feel the anger and events of yesterday boiling up again and have to shake my head to dispel the seething annoyance. I can't hide the beaming resentment in my eyes though.

He calls the specialist over and introduces us and I soon surrender to the situation and decide to accept and trust the man. After all, he *is* a doctor too, *with* the necessary qualifications. I am taken to a small room for the local anaesthetic, where my doctor takes my hand and the specialist and nurse prepare the equipment. "Don't you worry about anything," he assures me. "Everything will be okay. Just relax".

The specialist explains that he will take only three samples of tissue fluid from each breast, and shows me the areas he will take them from. While my doctor is preparing my arm for the local anaesthetic, the specialist announces that he is ready to start. My doctor inserts the needle. "It's okay," he assures me, looking me in the eye.

A movement behind him attracts my attention and through blurred eyes I see another man emerging to stand beside him. I blink to see clearly. I know this man from somewhere, I think to myself, as the local takes effect. Although he is indistinct, I am looking this man straight in the eye. I tell myself it is the medication that is causing confusion; it's as if I see the double of my doctor. The specialist starts with the left breast and talks to me as he removes the fluid. My eyes are following his hand now as I listen to his distant voice.

When all three samples are finally taken from the left breast, he reassures me that all is looking good. Then he slowly moves his hand towards my right breast. At that very moment I see a hazy hand appearing, that of the other man. It stretches out and takes hold of the specialist's hand. I watch in fascination. The mystical hand guides the specialist's hand to the far side of my right breast where the needle is finally inserted. The specialist looks at my doctor and says something inaudible to me. That is when I instantly drift off into a deep sleep.

When I wake up in the recovery room I can't stop thinking about the hazy hand and ponder the bizarre event all the way home. Every time I close my eyes I can see the shadowy hand guiding the specialist's hand to the correct spot. I keep telling myself that I know him from somewhere but I just can't put the pieces together.

A week later I visit my doctor for the test results. "Do you remember what happened and did you hear what we found?" he asks.

"No," I reply, wondering if he also saw the other man pull the specialist's hand right across to the far side of my breast.

"Well, you see, the specialist hit a lump on his first insertion on your right breast, and then I had to give you more anaesthetic to knock you out cold. But don't worry, the fluid tests are fine and you now need to see the specialist for further investigation of the lump."

I see the specialist, who examines me and admits to having been amazed at finding the lump so easily. "Although the mammogram didn't show any lumps and none of us could feel any lumps, the test results showed that the cells are a-typical, which means that we need to remove them as soon as possible." He explains the procedure and adds, "I will call you tomorrow and let you know when you need to be at the hospital. I just need to reorganise my schedule." I leave in a daze.

The next morning I am unable to concentrate on my work and begin to understand how women feel when they are told they have breast cancer. I suddenly understand what my aunt went through and feel really nervous. By lunchtime I have put myself through so much mental turmoil and, in a state, I grab my bag and car keys and flee to find some peace of mind. A woman colleague tries to stop me. She has noticed the state I am in and that I should not be driving.

I race off, not conscious of where I am going. My thoughts are in a muddle and the questions racing through my mind all want to know what lies ahead.

I find myself in a bookstore where I walk down the aisle of cards and around to the books. I stand in front of the bibles and other religious books and stare at the titles. I reach up on tiptoes to the top shelf and grab the first book my fingers touch: 'A guide for the advanced Soul', by Susan Hayward.

I flip the book open to a random page and my eyes fall on the following words:

'Accept your feelings of the moment, allow your inner strengths to carry you, put aside all questioning for today. Allow the day to reveal itself. Answers will flow through you in days to come. Believe the impossible, happiness will follow. The Buddha in the garden of Zen.'

What amazing words, I think, and just what I need to hear today. I read the front cover. It is a book of insight. In bold letters it says, "Hold a problem in your mind-open this book to any page and there will be your answer." Amazed at this event and completely taken aback by these words, I buy the book.

In my car I'm suddenly aware that I can't recall what route I had taken to arrive at this location. I realise I should not have been driving. Looking through the windscreen, I lean forward to place the key in the ignition.

A bee lands gently on the glass a mere half-metre from my eyes. The thoughts that went through my mind when my aunt departed now flow through my mind again. Peace floods my Soul as I recall how she insisted on showing me her scar from the removal of her breast. Great waves of peace and contentment flood over me. I am happy again. I am no longer afraid. I drive safely and slowly back to work, these words in the book stuck in my memory.

I find myself remembering them and repeating them over and over again. They are speaking so clearly to me. I know, from this moment, that there is nothing to worry about.

I arrive back in my office where my friend and boss are waiting. I don't even have to explain. They notice the difference in me.

I take out my new-found treasure book and go on to explain that these words I stumbled upon *really* spoke to me. I turn page after page but I can't find the words that I read. I am stunned. I write down the words and ask my friend if she can find the page. She can't either. I put the book aside and try to do some work.

Soon after, the specialist calls and tells me to be in theatre first thing in the morning. That evening, I continue searching for the words still so clear in my mind. "I really read them, I know I did," I explain to my husband. He also looks for the words I have now typed out, but they are nowhere to be found in the book. I feel as if I am going crazy.

"You *must* have read it, because I know that those are not your words," my husband assures me. "Perhaps it was from another book?"

I *know* I only picked up this one book. It remains a mystery how those words appeared before me on a page and then stuck in my mind so clearly. The next morning I undergo successful and peaceful surgery to remove the lump.

Self-Interpretation Of Hazy Hand

Relating to my own trauma of sexual abuse, I was overprotective with both my daughter and my son. I always put them first, worrying that they may also be sexually abused.

A-typical cells indicate cell progression towards cancer. So in interpreting metaphysical causation, as a preventative I began to actively take steps to release myself from my past experiences. I also began to re-order my patterns of thinking and created a mantra to encourage myself to love, approve of and accept myself more fully.

I had still not dealt with the mental and emotional trauma that was trying to communicate with me through illness. I did not fully understand, at this point, that it was the mind and emotions that caused physical illness.

I continued to remain silent about my sexual abuse and kept it from my parents and family. It was my secret and it was certainly eating at me. I believed that there was no merit in telling anyone something that happened when I was a child.

Be Aware

The 'benefit' of having experienced a specialist with such rude manners was certainly going to be a mental imprint-how not to relate to patients. It was good grounding for the day I was to qualify as a Reiki Master. I was learning how important it was to be sensitive to the unknown when consulting. However, in the here and now, he mirrored my rage and pushed all my anger buttons. He was extracting some of the deeply suppressed anger and hurt I had experienced from men. Not such a co-incidence that the specialist was a man, not a woman. Notice my fear and resistance to undressing for this male doctor. Imagine my thoughts, hurt and resentment with this doctor 'prodding' me, without caring whether I hurt or not.

The interaction of my spirit guide, again, was something most doctors and psychologists may have put down to the hallucinations of someone under local anaesthetic. That 'feeling' is something beyond the comprehension of most professionals.

Knowing today, as I do, that there truly is no such thing as co-incidence, I am convinced it can be ascribed to guidance and co-creation.

What were the odds of the specialist stabbing the needle into the very lump none of us knew existed, not even picked up on the mammogram (a creation of science)? I've 'been there' and have had the personal experience.

The mention of my hysterectomy during the appointment with the specialist was also noteworthy. This connected the underlying cause of the problem. Remember the inexplicable appearance of words on a page in a book? Was it my own powerful creation of inspiring words, or were my spirit guides sending me the words with powerful mental viewing? I have no explanation for this.

The bee appearing on my car window reminded me of my aunt and what she went through: it connected our breast problems and symbolically represented our spirit connection.

Chapter 9 - Psychic Awareness

(Approximate age 30, year 1998)

I am happily working as a financial secretary, reporting to the executive secretary. I have been trained to stand in for her when she goes on leave. My first day as her replacement, while she enjoys her leave, ends with great satisfaction as I get into bed. My dreams begin again.

I arrive at work early in the morning to catch up with my own work and still manage to have time to continue standing in for my boss. The two directors arrive at work early, and go on with their own duties. I sit back drinking a cup of coffee, satisfied with the amount of work I have done. I take a cup of coffee to each of the directors. The phone rings and I run to answer it. Simultaneously the managing director answers the phone; we are both on the line when we hear my boss's husband calling for help. He asks for his wife urgently. I talk first and say, "She is with you already, you are on holiday." There is silence on the other end. I hang up and walk back into the managing director's office. He, in turn, is still on the phone with a pained expression on his face. When I walk in, he sits down with his hand over his mouth and shakes his head. I sense something is wrong and call the other director with the news that something strange is happening. The managing director hangs up the phone and tells us both that my boss's husband is having a heart attack and that we need to get his wife home quickly. I turn and leave the office in a hurry to look for her, yet know she is not at work because she is on leave. The director finds her first and takes her home. I am shattered for the rest of the day, after learning that he died of a heart attack in hospital.

I wake up, disturbed and concerned. I know this is just a dream, yet I can't help feeling that this might be another one of those dreams of mine that come true. My day at work proceeds to absolute perfection. I had mastered the ability to choose to not dwell on the dream.

The dreadful day dawns, many months later. I have just given some documents to my boss and I return to my own desk. The call comes in, from her husband who asks her to come home. The director takes her home and they both take her husband to hospital.

Unfortunately, just as in the dream, he doesn't make it. He passes away from a massive heart attack. A cold shiver shudders through my entire body when I hear the news. I experience a fleeting feeling of anger toward myself. I do not understand why I keep dreaming about ominous events that come true and I wonder to myself if this is psychic awareness.

Self-Interpretation Of Psychic Awareness

The most powerful sign I saw, and understand today with this dream, was the form of communication I used, the telephone. My guides, my own Soul and my subconscious were sending clear information to me, for my own development, using the telephone as the medium. Of course the telephone is what we all rely on today for communication with someone who is distant and beyond our immediate physical contact. My senses were again strongly guiding me in the dream–communicating with me on a higher level. My boss's husband, having to make contact with her before his passing, used the telephone.

The speed with which I was completing my work in this dream was a positive indication of how quickly I was learning the true work I am supposed to be doing in this lifetime. My psychic awareness was opening fully, as reflected in my dreams.

Chapter 10 - Understanding

(Approximate age 31, year 1999)

I always seem to know when something is going to happen. Feeling disturbed about my continued dreams, thoughts and events that take place subsequently, I choose to visit a medium for a psychic reading.

Her confirmations shake and rattle me. I am told my intuition is very strong and she explains that I am receiving my information through dreams mostly, as I often block and pass off the intuition coming through my thoughts and senses during waking hours. She stresses the importance of following my intuition, as it is guidance and training for my own development. She also tells me that I am being trained in healing.

She goes on to introduce me to all my spirit guides who are with me at this moment: a Chinese man who is a fatherly figure, to teach and guide me into meditation and, later, feng shui. A Japanese doctor, teaching me the healing I am to do; a great-grandfather, who is always beside me, just to watch over me; a nun, who has been with me since I fell and injured my knee as a young child.

The woman giving me this information happens to teach meditation. She tells me later that I have been guided to her to learn how to meditate. I tell her how strange it is for her to say that, as I have recently been reading about meditation and searching for someone to teach me. I feel very attracted to learning meditation. She tells me a Chinese man in spirit has been guiding me forward to learn meditation, and it will prove to be a really important tool in my life.

I eventually start meditation. My first session brings with it a wave of sadness that washes slowly through me. I block this sadness as I come out of meditation. I don't want to cry in front of the group. That night I have the most horrific dream:

I am running around with a gun, shooting at the person who sexually abused me, screaming at him, shouting my anger at him, following through with many gun shots until he is full of holes. He must feel as I am feeling—full of holes.

In the dream I shout, "How do you feel with me shooting you for a change?" I finally collapse on top of a rock, exhausted and crying so many tears that a pool forms around my feet. When I wake up, there are real tears saturating my pillow.

During my third meditation lesson, she tells me my Japanese doctor wants to confirm that it was he I had seen after my hysterectomy operation and when the doctor discovered a breast lump. He now wants to consciously teach me healing, as he has been guiding me in healing in the astral plane, both when I am asleep at night and throughout my illnesses, for a long time.

Shock radiates through me on hearing this confirmation from a person who cannot possibly know of these events in my life. I reflect on how I, negatively, told myself I was losing my mind when I thought I had seen this spirit guide after my hysterectomy.

But here was the evidence, coming from someone else. Now, at last, I understand I have not lost my mind. I was guided. It was psychic awareness. Acceptance begins flowing through me.

I have always been reluctant to learn healing. I was self-conscious and too embarrassed to place my hands on someone else, worried I would look like some kind of a freak. I was far too nervous about doing this healing.

The following week everyone in our meditation group encourages me to do it, for the very first time. Self-consciously, I stand over one member of our group, not knowing what on earth to do. Our psychic medium explains that all I need to do is to relax. My spirit guide will lead the way for me. She urges me to go ahead and try it.

I take deep breaths, relax as if I were meditating, and off I go, placing my hands over different areas. Surprisingly, I feel my hands vibrating and the heat increasing. When I am through I find I, instinctively, have information for my 'patient'. No one is more amazed than me. I accurately diagnose two current problems that the 'patient' is aware of. I drive home completely absorbed with what I had accomplished. I am aware of how relaxed I was. It had felt so natural, once I started, as if I had always been doing this. I recall some of my earlier dreams where I remember placing my hands upon other people.

Each week at group meditation thereafter, I assist with healings. I expand and develop my confidence. I notice how many people are now coming forward to tell me of their ailments.

Despite these successes, I feel too uncomfortable to do healing outside our group. I become very close to three friends at work who eventually become my encouragement, my inspiration and guiding lights. They welcome all my healing attempts, boosting my confidence further. One friend joins our group to learn meditation. When our meditation teacher emigrated, my friend and I continue, for a short while, doing our meditations together. During one, she tells me "Tina, you are not in the right job, a personal assistant is not you. There is something more creative for you."

Her words are like music to my ears. I had been feeling unhappy in my career and was awakening to the fact that I was far more passionate about healing. I had an inner knowing that there was something more. Until then, I had ignored my thoughts and desires to do something different with my life.

Her words make a deep impression. As I recall them, they constantly remind me that there is something else for me to do. I'm just not sure what, exactly, or how to go about it.

My friends continue to encourage me with my healing. My passion has truly been awakened and continue to blossom. I gather many books and soak up all the teachings as time goes by.

Self-Interpretation Of Understanding

My true conscious healing had begun. My dream after my first meditation relating to the sexual abuse is easy to interpret. The gun is a symbol of aggression. Shooting someone means you feel aggression towards someone. The gun represents the male sexual organ. Holes represent a bad situation in life, one that we fear. The rock, again, is revealing one's inner strength to overcome the problem. At this time I was starting with the healing process. Anger was the first to emerge. I was obviously desperate to make the abuser feel as bad and sad as I felt. Coming out of the meditation I held back my tears, still fearful of revealing the secret I had held on to my whole life.

Crying in your dreams indicates a tendency to cover up your real feelings in your daily life. The pool of tears around my feet spoke of the deep emotional trauma in which I was stuck. See, too, how psychic my friend was, telling me I was in the 'wrong career'. We all have this psychic ability within us! It was not really the wrong career, but one that I had out-grown. My personal assistant career had served its purpose. We are always in the right place at the right time. But I was shifting towards a greater role and career.

Chapter 11 - Divine Timing

(Approximate age 32, year 2000)

After several visits to doctors and specialists and many different tests; in and out of hospital and a lot of frustration, no scientific evidence has been provided for how I am feeling.

I am very weak with too many symptoms to be taken seriously. Doctors are having a hard time believing me. No one knows what is wrong. I keep on meditating and doing my own healing. I know there is something wrong with my blood. I keep seeing little cartoon-like monsters. Just when I am ready to give up completely, the word 'bilharzia' enters, and sticks, in my mind. Is this what I have? I ask myself. I reason that I have had far too many blood tests for this to have been missed. Could it be? I convince myself it is impossible and push the thought from my mind.

Later that day my father asks if the doctors know yet what is wrong with me. I disappointedly reply, "No". His next words almost blow me off my feet: "Ask the doctor for a bilharzia test." I am shaken to my roots but still offer a debate: "Surely the blood tests would have picked it up by now?"

Besides, I am not aware of having been near a dam recently that could be infected with bilharzia. It all still seems highly unlikely.

However, I am desperate for some direction as I feel incapable of healing myself. I'm not even sure where to begin. I lack the confidence to follow my intuition.

The next day I ask my doctor to do a bilharzia test. My doctor sits in shock, hearing my words. He is mentally scanning and comparing my symptoms and those of bilharzia, and finally agrees that we should take another blood test to check. Although I am frustrated at yet more blood tests, I agree and am hopeful that this will finally be resolved.

Eventually the results arrive. Negative, no bilharzia present. Now I am really fed-up. What now? "No more tests," I say to myself, "I have had it." I leave, disappointed. I try really hard to convince myself that the doctors and scientific tests are right.

I am resting on the couch at home, weak, ill and depressed that no doctor is able to help me. I flick through the TV channels with the remote to take my focus off my illness. The first programme that catches my attention is about careers. They are stressing how important it is to follow through with a career where one's passion guides you, and not to become stuck in a career for money. What thought provoking inspiration this suddenly becomes. I marvel that I 'happen' to stumble onto this channel at this particular time. Is this just another co-incidence? While on the one hand I feel that my true passion for healing has been awakened, on the other I feel confused because I can't see how one can heal anyone when one does not even know the nature or the name of the ailment. I am well aware I have lost my passion for my career as a personal assistant. It is now just a job for money. I switch off the TV in disgust and move off to bed. The dreams continue:

I am in the middle of my dining room healing somebody who is lying on my dining room table. When I walk out to my veranda to say good-bye I see a display of white tablet bottles standing against the wall. I pick up three pointed, green leaves, joined at the stalk, and wonder where it has come from. I walk inside smelling the leaves and say out loud, "They smell like herbs of some kind". I place the leaves on the dining room table and sit at a desk. I wake up and don't pay too much attention to this vivid dream.

One week later my doctor calls and asks me to see him urgently. Quite mysteriously, another laboratory report has landed on his desk. Here was finally the unquestionable proof-I do in fact have bilharzia. The previous 'negative' report was incorrect, a mistake apparently. I sit, shocked, and recall part of another dream I had during the entire trauma when all the tests began. It was around the time I was being tested for leukaemia.

In the dream, my spirit guides were in a laboratory holding a piece of paper. When they left they took it with them. I remember that I smiled about it.

I now sit wondering if this was one of my psychic dreams. I hadn't remembered this dream until now, when it flashed through my mind. I remind myself that spirit guides assist us. Surely they would never hold back information, *unless* there was a reason? Perhaps, *now* was divine timing. I let go of these thoughts because I finally feel free, that we know for sure how I need to be treated.

My husband, Casey and Dustin need to be tested too. Casey and Dustin are okay, but my husband also tests positive. My true healing can now begin.

Self-Interpretation Of Divine Timing

Something most amazing becomes evident through the traumatic experience of medical tests in my life. Doctors and specialists are totally unable to help me. They truly do not know what is wrong with me.

I believe we are the only ones who can help ourselves, by guiding the doctors towards our aliment. No other human has your insight into your mind and body. Doctors cannot know everything about you unless they are in touch with, and trust, their intuition and psychic abilities. I am sure we all tell our doctors only of physical symptoms and nothing about our emotions. Then again, how many times have you told your doctor what is 'wrong' with you? Your body is talking to you all the time. You are guided all the time. The secret is to learn to listen. Be Aware!

An important learning tool for me was to trust my intuition and psychic abilities, because these are constantly pointing out reality.

Divine timing plays an important role. Here's the proof: in the week between the first bilharzia report (indicating a negative result) and the mysterious second (showing a positive result), I had gone through an amazing awakening period about my career, triggered by a TV programme. I realised I no longer wanted my present career. I honestly believed I had outgrown it and lost the passion to remain a personal assistant in the corporate world. I had gained the necessary experience to move on. My dream again illustrates my career and guides me directly to what is ahead for me.

My healing venue in my home is the area that was once my dining room.

·Consider, now, in terms of metaphysical causation theory: I was most certainly handing over my power to my male boss and others at work as I had been doing all my life. This 'giving away' began when, as a child, that most personal and intimate part of me was taken away removed from my control. Consequently I was locked into the belief that I was to keep giving my power away to please those around me. "That was how my life was and will continue to be," I believed, not understanding that I *retain* the power to, and can, change that belief. Until that point, I had not taken back my power and had never stood up for myself in any significant way.

Chapter 12 - Triggering Shifts

(Approximate age 32, year 2000)

I awake early in the morning. Soon it will be Christmas. It's a beautiful South African summer's day without a cloud in the sky. I am greatly inspired and motivated to take on a task I have been longing to do. I am about to transform my old orange-and-white tiled and carpeted bathroom into a special bathroom.

My husband mutters and moans, "Don't expect me to be any part of this. You want to do this, you do it yourself." I listen, smiling within, believing that he will help when he sees the big task unfolding. I'm not to know it yet, but, how wrong these thoughts are! I don't realise I will be doing this with my own hands, without his help.

I rush to get started, grabbing a bowl of cereal and proceeding to eat faster than ever before. Almost immediately, indigestion sets in. I gulp down a glass of vitamin supplement to assist my body with the physical energy it will need for this undertaking. I know that I need to be giving my body extra care and attention at this time, to assist the healing process it is undergoing. I am still very ill with bilharzia; the pain in my organs is ever present, my blood feels sluggish, my heart too weak, and my lungs struggle for breath. I have little energy and feel terribly drained all the time. Despite this, I am determined to transform my bathroom. I no longer want this orange bathroom with the same tile design of the bathroom in my childhood home. I had preferred those green tiles and feel that I have now outgrown this pattern too. I somehow don't vibrate with this colour. In fact, I hate it. I gather the necessary demolition tools and start by ripping up the carpet tiles.

Why would anyone put carpets in a bathroom? I ask myself. Perhaps the previous owners, elderly people, needed extra warmth–who knows?

The smell of old damp, dirt, urine stains and chemical cleaners leaps from the carpets and hits me like a slap in the face. Potty training took place in this bathroom. I feel nauseated by the smell and stand up too quickly. I find myself swaying and dizzy and the walls and floor appear to be floating around me. Stars are flashing everywhere and I feel heat rising. I place one hand on the tiled wall, one hand on my solar plexus. The coolness of the wall under my hand feels comforting, it contrasts to the heat within me. I feel secure now and lean my back against the firm, solid, cool wall. I breathe in and out slowly and deeply, gather my senses and allow my body to become still and steady.

I have more carpet squares to lift and wonder how I am going to face the stench that has been hidden under them for so long. I have started the job and know that I simply have to go on. There are no eager, helping hands around right now. While the family goes about preparing themselves for the day, I reach down more slowly this time and force myself to continue. I'm pulling up one carpet tile at a time with one hand while the other is holding my nose. Finally, all carpets are lifted, exposing a disgusting, bright red, cold, cement floor. I try to understand the previous owner's need for bringing in warmth with orange-toned, sand-coloured carpets.

I carry the refuse bag, bulging with old carpet tiles, outside. I take the time to breathe in fresh air and feel satisfied with my first accomplishment. I am proud of myself.

On return, I am met by an angry husband in the bathroom. He is shaking his head. "You're making a mess. You should have just left it."

He says goodbye and tells me that he is taking the children to spend the day swimming at his sister's home. I am shocked and angry. "Fine, go," I say, trying hard to suppress my annoyance.

Now I realise that he meant it when he said he wasn't going to help. I'm on my own. Helpless rage wells up in me and I angrily attack the walls, pulling and bashing the tiles and then smashing them on the floor. I am deeply engrossed in my thoughts and emotions as I vent my frustration on the wall tiles.

"How could he just go and have a nice relaxing day and leave me to do all the work? This isn't just my bathroom—it's his too. How spiteful and how lazy he is," I think to myself. He knows that I am not physically well enough nor am I am physically built for this type of DIY work. I don't know anything about renovating at this level.

"He doesn't love me or he would be here helping me," I reason. "We should be doing this together." I wallow in self-pity as I sit down on the edge of the bath.

I am exhausted and my tears are flowing. I also love swimming and would dearly love to be swimming now too, rather than doing this. I look at the half-tiled, half-destroyed walls and sigh. I realise with dread that I can't leave the bathroom like this. I started the work and I need to finish it. It was my idea and I need to take responsibility for it. I sit and pray quietly, asking God for guidance with this task. I had no idea what was involved in renovating a bathroom on my own. What was I thinking? I'm not a builder, I'm a personal assistant!

Shortly, I feel better and even inspired to continue removing the tiles from the wall. I feel the warm sun shining through the open bathroom window and soon have my usual smile back on my face. I make good progress when I find that the tiles are literally just falling off the wall with minimum effort. No real physical strength required-how easy this really is, and so much fun, too.

My mom comes down from her flat upstairs and peeps through the window to see how I am doing. "What a mess you've made," she comments. Suddenly I feel deflated again. Obviously there is going to be a mess, I think to myself. What would anyone expect? How can anyone expect to renovate without the temporary mess that goes with it?

"You have a lot of work ahead, but it will be worth it," she says and leaves me to my task. I get back to gently prying the tiles off the wall with the putty knife. As I listen to them falling, I feel a shift taking place in my subconscious. Although I don't know what it is, I just know instinctively that something is taking place within me.

My oldest brother, who is visiting for the Christmas holidays, comes downstairs and also peeps in the window to see what I am doing. "Oh no," he says, "you have a disaster on your hands. What were you thinking? Where is my husband and why isn't he helping you?"

His words make me instantly angry again. Of course I know what I am doing! What does it look like? I'm demolishing a bathroom. I inform him that my husband has conveniently taken the kids swimming for the day and that he wants no part of this.

"I can't blame him for getting out of this one," my brother replies, and smugly walks away, leaving me smouldering once more. Why did he have to bring up my husband's part in this? I tell myself to stop all the mind chatter and focus on what I need to be doing.

I become totally absorbed in removing all the tiles, and all the while thoughts and emotions well up inside me. I recall distant and long suppressed scenes of sexual abuse by an older male. This is so strange; I consciously connect the colours of orange and red to the chakra zones of the body. I connect the stench still in the air from the carpets to smells deeply ingrained in my subconscious. In their similarity they serve as catalysts to trigger my healing.

Now I begin to realise what is taking place within me and continue with the flow of thoughts and emotions as the tiles peel away from the wall. Finally I sit back on the edge of the bath for a breather and find that I am feeling much better. Good, in fact. I have removed all the tiles, but look what the walls look like now! Chipped and cracked and definitely not the smooth, ready-to-paint walls I expected.

I now have to plaster up the holes, but there are so many. I rub my fingers across some areas only to find the plaster crumbling under my touch. "Oh no," I groan. "Now this is really a disaster." Maybe I could just re-tile these walls. Not what I want to do and also not the finished picture I have in mind. I want to paint, not tile. I mix some plaster and start applying it to the walls, knocking off the loose plaster as I go. A big hole suddenly appears as a huge slab of plaster breaks away, revealing the red brick behind it. I sit back on the bath again and sigh. I hate problems. Why couldn't this wall just be smooth? Why do I have to find a hole? Damn!

A fierce anger builds up in me and once again I feel my body changing with the emotion. I kick the pile of tiles strewn on the floor in anger and yelp in pain as a corner of a sharp tile cuts into my big right toe. I grab my toe as the pain shoots through my body and I swear as I kick off my sandal to rinse my toe in the basin. "Serves you right for wearing sandals and becoming so violent with your anger, doesn't it," I tell myself angrily. The healer within me starts to focus loving, caring thoughts into my hands, which are cradling my injured toe.

The bleeding doesn't stop immediately and I'm surprised at the amount of blood coming out of my toe. I hobble to the bathroom cupboard and find a plaster. I hobble back to the basin, leaving a trail of blood over the tiles on the floor. With my foot back in the basin I now have blood squirting out like a fountain. I also have blood all over my hands as I try to stop the bleeding. Now the thought crosses my mind that I have bilharzia in this blood that I am touching. I am actually touching bilharzia! What a remarkable thought. Well, if I can touch it, why can't I heal it? I ask myself. With these thoughts I run cold water gently over my toe, which continues to bleed profusely. I wonder to myself why it is that my husband, who also had bilharzia, is now bilharzia-free. My bilharzia is chronic and the medication has not cleared it. I'm now suddenly aware of the choice of words going through my mind. '*My*' bilharzia. Why on earth do I want to call it '*mine*'? For heaven's sake-it is a dis-ease caused by a parasite–it is not, and never will be, *mine*!

I shift my thought process and say out-loud: "I no longer choose to own bilharzia. It is not mine. I no longer want this. I let it go with the flow of this blood. I let it go." At that moment I remember that I had forgotten to take the repeat treatment of medication to kill the bilharzia. I need to repeat it, as the first dose did not completely kill the parasites. I know within that I have avoided the medication because of the side effects I experienced the first time. What will be next if this dose doesn't work either? I shake that negative thought right out my mind and replace it with a positive utterance: "it *will* work this time," I tell myself confidently.

I promise myself that I will take those tablets tonight; I'm now ready to take on what is ahead. I dry my toe and quickly apply a plaster. The thought crosses my mind that I am now applying plaster to my body instead of the walls. How ironic, I think. If only applying plaster to walls was as easy as applying it to the body.

I finally face the fact that I have a big hole in the wall that needs cement and not plaster, and suddenly feel weak again. When will it end?

I leave the bathroom and take a break. I eat and drink slowly, paying close attention to my body, which I have been neglecting. I relax on the couch with my throbbing foot raised against the wall to stop the bleeding. The blood is still oozing through the plaster that is now saturated. I close my eyes and allow myself to rest, rewarding my body for the hard work I have accomplished so far. The house is so silent. There is no one around and I revel in the peace.

In this blissful interlude, I suddenly become aware of a change of vibration in energy around my toe–a warm glow spreading through the wound. I feel comforted and at peace. I know that my doctor spirit guide is present and carrying out healing on my toe. I drift off into a peaceful and deep sleep for half an hour.

When I wake up I am refreshed, filled with love, peace and inspiration-and ready to go back to the bathroom. I know the wisest thing to do is clear up the broken tiles on the floor and in the bath. I first remove the blood-saturated plaster, rinse my toe again and apply a new plaster. Then I put on a soft slipper. Everyone was right, what a mess!

I throw all the broken tiles into the dustbin. The room now feels clean. A far better energy is present with the clutter cleared out.

I have no idea how to mix cement, so I decide to plaster the hole instead. "Plaster will just have to do," I tell myself. I spend the rest of the day plastering with care and love, all the time feeling the growing emotion of fear in my stomach as the time approaches to take the medication.

It is evening and the family has still not arrived home. I clean up in the bathroom and take a relaxing bath, admiring the plastered walls and all the progress made. I day-dream about the effect I want to create in this bathroom. Walls will be sponged, a new technique I have learned. I have chosen colours that need to blend well, a blue-grey, another lighter blue-grey and a pale green. I just know I am going to enjoy this new bathroom. I climb out of the bath, totally exhausted, and fall into bed. The family finally arrive home and I fall asleep.

I awake the next morning with a heavy, burning sensation of fear in my stomach. I am immediately aware that I forgot to take my medication again! I eat breakfast and take the medication right away, telling myself I can no longer run away from this and must face it.

I ask my husband to please help me remove the porcelain soap dish, toilet-roll holder and the old metal cabinet. These are things I just physically cannot do. I tell him that he needs to cement the wall afterwards. He grumpily agrees to do it for me.

I am grateful for his help and when he gets busy I sense the anger rising in him as he battles to remove the soap dish. I recall my own anger, feelings and thoughts that took place in this bathroom the day before. I leave him to be alone with his own experience.

I am feeling weaker as the medication is being absorbed in my body. The pain grows in the pit of my stomach as it is so unsettled. I rest on the bed meditating for a while. The medication begins ripping my stomach lining to pieces; the pain has brutal strength over me. I break into a cold sweat. Holding my stomach with my legs curled to my chest, I battle to breathe.

Nausea rises fast and furious, I am unable to move. "I can't vomit," I think. "I can't walk to the toilet, I dare not vomit." I can't take much more of this, I tell myself. I am trying to take large deep breaths to feed my lungs and brain with precious oxygen to get through this. Then, mercifully, the pain slowly subsides. Waves of nausea continue washing over me like the restless waves of the ocean. My head starts pounding while my stomach cramps wax and wane, riding with the waves of nausea. Hot tears are flowing and their warmth, trickling over my face, feels soothing against the background of pain that is racking my body. I'm fascinated by the thought of feeling comforted by my own tears. I feel a cleansing of childhood memories taking place. I force my thoughts to more positive things and breathe in and out slowly and deeply.

All the time I am praying for help and guidance through this process. I focus on going within.

I settle into a visual meditation, watching particles of medication being absorbed in my blood. I recall the blood I was touching the day before and relive the thought that I can heal whatever I can touch. I see the medication fighting the parasite of bilharzia within. I travel with the medication in my blood through all the veins, in and out of my heart. I stop at my stomach and consciously send streams of divine love to every cell that forms part of my stomach. I breathe crystal clear golden yellow light deep into the cells and affirm deep healing is taking place. I thank each and every cell for undergoing the pressure and stress caused by the medication. I see my hands, very small and within my stomach, smoothing, clearing and vibrating warmth, love and light deep inside. I re-enter my blood, connecting with the medication and healing each cell of blood with white divine love as I mentally pass through the tunnels of my own veins. I turn my attention back to my heart and sit within the chamber, listening to the sound of blood flowing, the pumping so loud within, yet so silent on the outside. I fill my heart with love, joy and peace and affirm that I let go and accept good health from here onwards. I am consciously aware of the presence of my body from the outside.

The pain eases, the nausea has gone and my head is vibrating gently. The warmth that surrounds me is peaceful, soothing and relaxing. I take a deep, long breath, hold it and then slowly let it go. I open my eyes with the inner knowledge that the bilharzia has been taken care of!

I return to the bathroom, grateful to see my husband has removed everything I asked him to. Now, big, deep, ugly holes are the result of his efforts. I remember hearing the banging on the walls and realise I somehow related the banging on the walls to the pounding of my heartbeat. I feel stronger, yet aware of the unsettled feeling in my colon.

Moments later, intense pains once again take hold of me. "Not again!" I groan. By now I know that diarrhoea is sure to follow shortly, all just side-effects of the medication. I painfully walk to the lounge to find my husband settled in front of the TV. I ask if he is going to cement in the holes. "Yes, but not today," he shouts. I'm annoyed and return to the bed to rest. Again gripping pains destroy my rest. I now desperately have to go with the flow. Seated on the toilet, I gaze around at these big holes. I feel like giving up this whole renovation and calling in professionals.

Later, feeling better, I focus on sanding down my unprofessional plastering. I get the inspiration to use the drill with a sanding disk, rather than self-sanding as it is weakening my body. I gather the drill and sanding disks and notice my husband shaking his head in annoyance. I ignore him and tell myself that I am capable of doing this alone. I am soon to discover that I have no strength to undo the drill for attaching the sanding disk. I sheepishly venture into the lounge and ask my husband to loosen and re-attach the sanding disk. I was trying so hard to avoid his annoyance, but now simply grin and bear it.

I start sanding the walls and soon find myself caked in a cloud of dust with the ever-increasing heat of the drill in my weary hands. My arms are aching and feel ready to drop off. I take a break, coughing and choking as the dust congests my breathing and fills my lungs. I know this is not wise; my lungs are already weak from bilharzia. I find myself a mask and goggles and continue taking frequent breaks throughout the day, with many thoughts relating to sanding and smoothing areas of my life.

I am greeted the next morning with the beautiful, special sound of birds chirping happily as they move about their own morning routine. My body is peaceful and rested.

My husband, thankfully, goes ahead and cements all the areas that will now take some time to dry completely. I keep myself busy by touching up and plastering areas where my pressure on the drill created deep grooves. I take the day in my stride, giving a good deal of attention to my body and thoughts. I wonder how many parasites were killed off, and finally feel quite confident that they have all gone. Later I sand down the plastering and clean up all the dust. I have a fairly presentable bathroom under renovation. Tomorrow is Christmas Day, my day off, and a day to relax with family around my sister-in-law's pool.

Christmas blissfully comes and goes. It is now time to complete this bathroom before New Year. My body is in a good vibration and feels healthier than it has in a very long time. My energies are also picking up and I know this must mean the bilharzia is sure to be cured.

I take the repeat blood tests to check. I have to wait patiently for two weeks to get results. In the interim I move on and start painting the bathroom. It is a long, difficult process, especially for a short person on the top of a stepladder. I spend all day painting and focus on monitoring the thoughts flowing through my mind with each stroke of the roller. I allow myself time to ride with the flow of emotions connected to all these thoughts. I know how important it is to release suppressed emotions. This is all part of my healing process. I now know that I needed to do this task alone to bring about the necessary healing. I am far more understanding of my husband's initial choice not to be involved.

The following day I wake up with the awareness of a deep inner strength that hasn't been present for a very long time. I don't have to force myself to work in the bathroom. The eagerness and inspiration is bubbling within naturally. I sit in front of my bedroom mirror totally absorbed at how different I look this morning. A major shift has taken place. I am so proud of the journey I have allowed myself to take. I am so grateful for the guidance and assistance from God and my guides through it all.

With painting all complete, my husband miraculously agrees to tile the bathroom floor and to attach the new soap dish, toilet roll holder and mirrors. I sit on the edge of the bath in total satisfaction. A difficult journey of healing and manual labour is over. It has been well worth it!

Days later my doctor calls me to his rooms. "You are officially bilharzia-free, your blood is clear," he cheerfully tells me. A burst of bubbling laughter and smiles are my instant responses. All the pain and hurt was worth it after all. It is finally over.

Self-Interpretation Of Triggering Shifts

I chose to renovate my bathroom in the midst of going through healing from bilharzia.

The bathroom itself represents the purification, water also being the symbol of emotions. The toilet is symbolic of sexual organs and the release and flushing of the required emotions. The colour orange is the colour of the energy vibration of the sacral chakra in your body, connected to sexuality and the ability to give and receive. It represents the energy development of the years 7 through 14. How significant that I should have been guided to buy this house that had exactly the same bathroom tiles as the house of my early childhood. Note my childhood house had green tiles, green matching to the heart chakra of the energy vibration in your body. The childhood house was a memory trigger of the time when the actual sexual abuse took place. The green tiles indicated heart-breaking emotions and experiences for me. I had truly been robbed of my joy way back then. This time, however, I was able to deal with the past trauma. Notice how my husband leaves me to do this renovation with my own 'hands'. A potent choice of words for a hands-on healer! Of course all the anger and suppressed emotions are destined to come out during this renovation. The stench from the carpets was the exact smell needed to trigger and awaken the shifting of my memories in my subconscious. Here the **_smell_** I recalled from the sexual abuse was so deeply ingrained in me. The smell created nausea.

The nausea I suffered indicated that I was trying to avoid-reject the healing I needed to be doing from sexual abuse.

Clearly, I really did not want to confront the sexual abuse and the associated emotions that were trapped with it. It was my past, after all, and long gone. Another amazing so-called 'co-incidence': beneath the orange carpets was a cold, red, cement floor-red being the base root chakra, representing the energy development of years 1 through to 7. Now sexuality does fall into the orange area, but it is through the root, the red chakra, that sex takes place. Here is the connection: colours carry healing vibrations, which immediately and automatically bring about healing to the associated chakra, whether you know anything about healing or not. So the colour vibrations were assisting the healing process, without my awareness. And, of course, the red just channelled my healing off into the depths of what had remained hidden and suppressed within me for all these years.

The positive inspiration coming from my mom, "You have a lot of work ahead, but it will be worth it," quite amazingly told me how this healing would be worth it. I brought the mention of my career into this experience, clearly showing how both my career and sexual abuse linked together and resulted in one illness. The new painting techniques I was experimenting with were also connecting to my new career techniques, essentially creativity. I was surely being guided in the direction of the art of feng shui. The colour I chose for the walls, blue-grey, was most significant: the blue triggered the communication chakra at the throat and grey indicated blockages. Progressing into green, there is the healing of the heart. I was re-asserting myself and acknowledging my 'power' in a fundamental transformation. It was all working together wonderfully for me to heal myself. Divine alignment!

Chapter 13 - Work From Home

(Approximate age 33, year 2001)

An advert from my post box falls from the pile in my hand onto my desk at home. It says "R35,000 a month part time!" A work-from-home business opportunity. I sit and ponder this ad, wondering if I should follow it up. I choose to ignore it and throw it in my small dustbin under my desk. The following day my maid takes the advert out of the dustbin and places it back on the desk. My husband reads through it and suggests we look into it. I stick it to the wall but give it no further heed.

My husband finally responds to the ad and we later join to start our own work-from-home business selling nutritional products. When the first products arrive, I immediately recognise the three-leaf pointed logo on the white bottle, and remember my past dream about working-from-home.

I start using the products just in time to boost my energy levels to where they should be for a cycling race. I have been struggling with fatigue since recovering from bilharzia and battling to get back to my normal cycling strength. The long and the short of it is that my health greatly improves and I am amazed. I go on to lose weight I gained during my childbearing years and feel and look greater than ever before.

Self-Interpretation Of Work From Home

This is where the other part of my new career comes directly into focus, the white bottles and herbs I saw in my previous dream (chapter 11), become relevant. The nutritional supplements help me to change my physical body and I feel like a new person-I am undergoing dramatic, beneficial change.

Chapter 14 - Following Guidance

(Approximate age 33, year 2001)

My husband goes away on business to Germany for four weeks. I want to attend a function on our nutritional products and think about it all day. I am in two minds as to whether I should go at all: great indecisiveness fills my thinking and I feel unsettled. I think about using my husband's company car because it is safer than mine and needs to run to keep the battery charged. I tell myself that it is a silly thought because my own new car is obviously safe too–perhaps not as strong as his, but safe all the same.

When evening comes, I make the decision to go, but I will go in my own car. As I prepare, I notice my stomach tightening with inexplicable dread. I ask myself what the cause for the fear could be and then again think about using husband's car. No, I decide with resolve; I will use mine, and that's final. I walk up to my car, take my keys out of my bag to open my door and discover that I am holding husband's car keys and not my own.

I stop momentarily, feeling a cold shudder run through my body. I immediately reason with myself that I must have chosen those keys for a specific reason and should not ignore it. I climb into his car and can't shake a lingering, uncomfortable feeling. I put on a CD, 'The Best of the Carpenters', to help me relax and to soothe my fear. I am in no rush, having allowed plenty of time to arrive at the function.

It had rained earlier in the day, the roads are wet and traffic on the highway is congesting slowly. We sit bumper-to-bumper, as the evening shadows lengthen, and still sit there when darkness sets in. When the traffic suddenly clears in the fast lane I quickly change lanes and begin moving past the stationary traffic. Just as I breathe a sigh of relief and settle at comfortable speed, the truck ahead of me slams on his brakes. I hit the brake pedal too and see him swerve aside into a neat little space in the slow lane, leaving me skidding towards the stationary vehicle that fills my windscreen. Braking too late, I crash right into the back of the stationary Porsche. "No, no, no!" I scream in frustration and disappointment and find myself shaking uncontrollably. My head is spinning and I have suddenly forgotten what to do in the event of an accident.

An angry man climbs out of his Porsche and approaches me. His look speaks volumes about the rage and verbal abuse that is about to burst forth from his irate frame. I am petrified and refuse to open the window as he raises his fist to smash the glass. At that moment a mysterious hand out of nowhere falls on his shoulder and a big tow-truck driver turns him away from my car. Where did he come from; how did he get there so quickly? He takes the angry Porsche owner back to his car and calms him down. Was this an angel? I sit in chilly silence, tears rushing down my face. I am frightened and feel terribly alone. A desperate wave of emotion passes over me and I wish husband were here right now and not in Germany.

Finally, the tow-truck driver approaches me. I am still fearful, in shock and shaking uncontrollably. He encourages me to open the window and puts his hand on my shoulder and squeezes gently. "Are you alright?" he asks. I can't find my voice, so I nod instead. When I open the door his next words hit me like a sledgehammer; "Lady, you're lucky to be driving this big, strong car and not one of those small runabout cars". You could have knocked me over with a feather! Where did this come from? This man has no clue that I own and drive a one of those small cars, so why would he use that very make of car when he speaks to me, especially when he appears out of nowhere and so mysteriously. How close I came to driving in my own car today did someone put those keys in my hand? Did it happen by design rather than by accident? Absolutely! A higher hand is leading me. My tears of gratitude and wonder could not be contained.

The mystery man tells me that we need to move my car out of the traffic before someone else rams into my car. The angry Porsche owner is still fuming as he paces up and down, fists tightly clenched. I am guided across all the lanes of traffic to the tow-truck, where this kind man settles me into his truck. He offers to call an ambulance for me, but I tell him that I'm alright and just need to regain my composure. I sit in silence, listening to the drone of the slow moving traffic next to me and thank God again that He ensured that I take my husband's car today. As my eye catches the angry man in the middle of the traffic I also thank God for placing the tow-truck man, or should I call him the 'angel', right there to keep me from being beaten up by the furious man. I sit wondering if this is all real. Was this driver sitting, waiting for me to arrive on the scene? Possibly. Anything is possible where God has a plan in a person's life.

Finally, with my husband's smashed car hooked to the back of the tow-truck, we head off to the police station nearby. Here, the moment arrives where I have to stand face to face with the angry, violent-looking man. Mercifully, the gentle tow-truck driver escorts me into the station. The other driver is still pacing up and down with clenched fists. Suddenly the man cannot hold it in any longer and turns to me in a rage. "You stupid, dumb blonde! What were you thinking, woman? I have just got my car back, today, from the panel-beaters. It has taken months to fix and now you come along and smash it up again! Don't you blondes know where the brakes are? You're going to pay for this, woman, you're going to pay!" He is screaming now and I step back in fear. The tow-truck driver moves between us and forcibly pushes the raving man away from me. "She is in enough shock. Don't even attempt to push it. It was an accident. Accept it and get over it." The policeman runs around the counter and helps to drag the man away from me. They take the man outside and warn him to not make the matter worse.

Another policeman approaches the counter and asks me to complete the forms. My hand is shaking so much that I can't write. The tow-truck driver takes the pen and helps me to fill in all my details. I can't even think straight. I can hardly tell them who I am! What is happening here? I'm in a total panic.

The policeman and the tow-truck driver think of calling an ambulance because of the degree of my shock, but I dissuade them, telling them that I will soon be myself again. I dread being at the mercy of an uncaring specialist again and concentrate on deep breathing. I reach into my bag and hand them my ID.

I finally gain a sense of control and give all my details. I have to explain that it is in fact my husband's company car. I urgently want to get home because I feel completely exhausted, but hear that I have to wait for this angry man to make his statement and exchange details for insurance purposes. When the first policeman escorts him back into the charge office, he is much calmer. He completes his form and we exchange details.

The tow-truck driver is giving me a ride home and tells me again how lucky I am to have been in a big strong car. He tells of the many people he has found with terrible chest and leg injuries from the steering wheels and pushed-back engines of what he calls 'those small runabout cars'. He goes on to point out that because I am extremely short, I could have been terribly hurt since I sit so close to the steering wheel. When I ask him how he came to appear on the scene so quickly, he tells me there were several accidents in that very spot that very morning and that he just happened to be waiting for another one to happen in what he called that 'very likely spot'. I realise now just how guided and protected I was. I don't have the energy to speak very much and when he insists, in his over-protective manner, on walking me to the door, I watch for his reaction when he sees my car. I am not disappointed. When he lays eyes on my small blue runabout car in the driveway he stops short in his tracks and puts both hands over his mouth. Now he too understands the divine intervention that has taken place.

My parents come down from their flat with my children and I let the tow-truck driver explain what happened. On leaving, he gives my car one, long last look and shakes his head in total wonder and disbelief. A good man–but then again, aren't all angels good?

My parents hold me, hugging me as I break down in tears. I am weak and tired and ask them to leave me as I need to phone my husband. My children go upstairs to spend the night with my parents and I go into the lonely house. Fear twists in my stomach because I have to break the bad news to my husband. I send a message over the internet asking him to contact me urgently.

He calls within minutes and I tell him, in sobbing tears, what happened. His reaction is almost as bad as that of the driver of the Porsche. He rants and raves and scolds and asks me why I used his car. His company is going to be furious.

Two very irate men in one day venting their anger at me! Instead of his arms around me, he is on the other side of the world and he is terribly annoyed. At me! Perhaps the distance between us is another blessing, I tell myself, and I try to find some composure. He adds insult to injury when he tells me that I had better contact his company and that I need to sort 'this mess' out with them. He wants nothing to do with it. He adds that his car had better be ready for him when he returns from Germany. He ends the call in anger and I sit stunned for a long time, wondering how so much could go wrong in such a short time.

I call someone from his company to sort out the car in the morning. He is objective enough not to rant at me too and takes down all the details. To my surprise he then tells me not to worry and assures me that he will sort it out and that I need not give it another thought. He has the decency to ask if I was hurt or injured in any way, and if there is anything he or the company can do for me. How nice of him. I decline his offer of further help and hang up. My legs are ready to give in. I get a grip on myself and take a bath. I just want to sleep. I climb into bed, crying, and when I close my eyes I see the accident repeatedly taking place in my head. I open my eyes and shake my head, but I can't escape the vivid images as they flash through my mind. Finally, unable to sleep I get out of bed and walk around the house.

Strangely, I now experience my own anger beginning to simmer deep within me. I have more questions than answers. How can my husband be more concerned for the welfare of his car than that of his wife? The anger is forcing its way up now and I lash out, shouting the frustration in violent words in the empty house, aimed towards him. I go back to bed and try to meditate, but I can't. I sit crying all night, unable to sleep, my head pounding painfully when I try to rest, my eyes swollen from crying. When morning finally arrives I am slightly calmer, yet still shaking. I can't stop my body from shaking. I take another bath and am grateful when my mom offers to take the children to school. I call my office and explain that I won't be in today. I try to eat, but I feel like vomiting and push the food aside. I drink some water and go back to bed. I try to relax and meditate again and find that I still can't stop my body shaking. It's as if I just cannot settle. In sheer desperation, I call my doctor, and ask for a tranquiliser to calm me down. Mercifully he sends it to me. Later in the day, people from my husband's company, who I have never met, call and ask if there is anything they can do for me. They encourage me not to worry about the car and tell me that all has been taken care of. Many people from my office call and ask if they can do anything for me. Finally, feeling just a little more loved, I relax on the bed and fall asleep for most of the day.

I wake up in the evening, feeling more refreshed. A measure of calm has been restored.

Now I can think more clearly about the event. How truly blessed I was. How glad I am that I followed my guidance and how grateful I am for the fact that 'someone' had made me take the 'wrong' car keys. I was taken care of. Someone was directing my steps and my doings–for sure. What a gem that tow-truck 'angel' was! How lucky I am to have so many caring people, (even though, mostly strangers) around me, phoning me and reaching out to help me, when I could not help myself.

Self-Interpretation Of Following Guidance

This experience illuminated the problem I have with communication. I had great resistance to attending the function as I knew they would randomly choose people to come up on stage and share their experiences.

The driver of the Porsche displayed that he has a repeated attraction of accidents with his car.

My guides, still busy enlightening me to their guidance, were now starting to get through to me. What a thrilling miracle. "They must be dancing with joy in heaven," I thought!

The tow-truck driver followed his own intuition and guidance to be there for me. Thankfully!

My husband experienced his own anger and fear as he reacted to my experience. I realised, too, that the distance between my husband and me was manifesting on levels other than the geographical (between South Africa and Germany).

Caring people are always around.

Chapter 15 – Challenging Decisions

(Approximate age 33, year 2001)

I have achieved everything I set out to do in the corporate world. I am now dissatisfied with my life as a personal assistant for one of the biggest companies in the country. I know I have outgrown this role. This had been my ultimate career goal to date, with the title I chose for myself. When my boss offered me the position of "executive secretary" I accepted, requesting that the title be "personal assistant" instead. At the time, little did I realise what was truly coming with the title I chose.

I had, privately, become a person developing into healing and assisting many people at work on a personal level-a much wider scope than the original intention of this title. Now, no longer passionate about being a corporate personal assistant, I carefully note and acknowledge that my life is taking a new direction. I am also working part-time selling nutritional products, and I'm really passionate about helping people with healing in their lives. I so desperately want to do hands-on healing and share good quality nutritional ideas with every person who comes my way. I wonder if I could really give up my 'safe' and 'easy-to-fall-back-on' personal assistant career to take charge of this new direction that is beckoning me so strongly. Fear leaps within me each time I ponder changing my career for something that could possibly not match what I am earning.

How would my husband and children take this news? How would other people react to me if I were to really tell them who I am, what I desire to be doing and what I truly feel and believe to be a part of my Soul purpose in this life? Many feelings distract me from wholehearted, committed work in the office and I am depleted of energy. I have been relying on the nutritional products to keep me moving, but late this particular afternoon I feel too ill to continue working. I am desperately tired.

I visit my doctor and when he has done his probing and preliminary tests, he suspects a bleeding ulcer. He orders a G-scope, which confirms a bleeding ulcer. I settle at home with a herbal aloe remedy and hands-on healing, as well as my doctor's medication.

I take myself through deep, Soul-connecting meditations, working through and ensuring that the career move I want to make is the right one and will move me forward in life. Each meditation becomes stronger and more meaningful, confirming I am moving in the right direction.

My strength, faith and confidence is building and I daydream every waking hour about my own home business where I am helping so many people who are sent to me for help. One week later, still recovering from my bleeding ulcer, I force myself to accomplish a fitness challenge that I have set for myself. I'm going to do the 94.7 Cycle Challenge in Johannesburg, South Africa. I ask my doctor to encourage and support me, and to give me go-ahead to cycle. My colleagues and team cyclists strongly recommend that I don't cycle, probably because they know I have not done any road training. The only fitness training I have done, in fact, is a couple of hours in the gym on a spinning bike. But I feel totally adequate with my nutritional supplements, my natural healing techniques and a strong positive attitude. I am going to do it.

I'm excited-and somewhat anxious-as I stand shivering in the cool, overcast weather on this early morning at the start line. I am aware of the many healthy and fit cyclists around me and I try to convince myself that I am as fit as they are. I know that in many ways I'm not alone on this journey.

When we set off, my first large hill approaches on the horizon. With my head down, I'm totally focused and prepared for this climb, my mind on my pedal strokes and my breathing. Sweat is pouring from me as I finally reach the top. On the other side, I descend fast and freely with no effort other than keeping myself balanced on my bike. With the high speed of the descent, my body shivers uncontrollably in the cold wind and I can feel my muscles stiffening. Oh no, I think, I need to warm up my muscles again.

Eventually, on the level ground further on, I lean into the strong pedal strokes and immediately feel the warmth returning, only to look up and see another hill approaching. This is where I decide to shift focus completely-away from what is ahead, back to the pleasant downhill with the cold wind that I was grumbling about a few minutes earlier. I notice how quickly the condition of my muscles alters, from each laborious climb to the next extremely welcome free-wheel.

I decide to channel my thoughts to the similarities between this marathon cycle challenge and my anticipated career change. Would I truly have the courage to make such a dramatic change in my life? I decide to put this cycle race on par with my life challenge. "If I make it to the end of this race then I will change my career," I tell myself. I continue to make my strenuous way over many hills, muscles cramping, jumbled thoughts flashing and lingering and each time having to take mental control of my situation.

Almost at the halfway mark, another hill looms in front of me. My legs are now terribly stiff and sore and I decide that I am not going to make it. I just can't take another hill. I climb off my bike and painfully take on this challenge on foot, envious of all the other people passing by so fast and apparently pain-free. After a long dreary march I reach the top. I put my bike down and head immediately for the massage tent. A young man settles me down and starts oiling and massaging my painful legs. The pain is so excruciating that I am ready to give-up. I ask him when the next pick-up truck will be coming by, as I don't want to finish this race.

He stops massaging for a brief moment and promptly says, "You are not going to give-up that easily. If you want me to continue massaging your legs then you have to continue cycling." I involuntarily nod my head and agree. Yes, I will ride—even though I know it is only for the massage that I will do it. In the back of my mind I have the escape hatch wide open: if push comes to shove, I will ride a short distance and then stop and wait for the truck.

He continues to massage and jokingly tells me that he has magical hands and that when he is finished with me, there will be no more pain. I am well aware of the benefit my legs are getting from his skilled hands and wonder again at the magical healing touch humans can develop. I wonder if he really understands that what he is saying to me is not a joke at all. I just relax, say nothing more and allow him to finish his task. On completion he again insists that I finish the race before he turns to another person needing a massage.

I collect my bike and one of my fellow teammates and colleague calls me on my cell. "Where are you?" he asks, calling from the finish line. "I'm at the massage tent and going to wait for the pick-up truck," I explain. "No", he insists. "You are past the worst part of the race. From where you are it just gets easier– keep going". His spark of positivity finally penetrates and I realise that I will probably reach the finish line quicker than sitting waiting for the truck. I climb on to my bike and to my own surprise I have no pain at all. My legs are perfect once again. My energy and inspiration peak. "Okay, let's do this, Tina," I encourage myself. I find many other people sitting on the side of the road as I go by with a smile. My focus is now firmly on the finish line. I don't stop again, passing all the water points, armed only with good nutrition and a positive attitude. Amazingly, I have the strength to ride the very last hill, passing plenty of people who are walking painfully up the steep incline. The exhilarating joy is indescribable when I finally reach the finish line. Tears of joy streak my face as emotions flow. The only negative is regret that my husband is not there to see me achieve one of my greatest goals to date.

When I walk up to receive my medal, I remember what I agreed to do; to change my career on completion of this race. Walking beside my bike with my medal, my legs begin aching again. My boss's wife walks up to congratulate me. She says she has been waiting to see me make it. A wave of guilt sweeps over me, knowing that I am considering giving up working with her husband to take on my Soul career.

I allow myself a few more weeks to ensure I am confident enough to resign and that my decision is a good one. When the time comes, I type my letter of resignation, feeling a huge tug and shift within me as I do it. But I am not quite ready to sign the letter of resignation. I leave it for the weekend, taking a lot of time in thought and meditation.

Monday morning comes and I dress for work, pick up my letter and decided it is time to 'just do it'. I sign it and tell my husband that it's done. My husband accepts my decision with a great deal of apprehension. That morning I go ahead and hand my boss my letter of resignation. The news soon spreads throughout the company. I feel a huge relief, as if someone has lifted a large burden from my shoulders. Everyone notices this major change in me and in my spirit. I am leaping and skipping in excitement and bottled-up energy. The worst is over. My new future and the passion I feel for it are beckoning.

Self-Interpretation Of Challenging Decisions

It is important to note how, through this event, I again put others before myself. This was my problem in my career up till now; I wasn't doing all the work for myself any longer, it was for someone else-and just for money. I don't have to be concerned how others might react; it is my life and my career.

I was, however, out of step and uncomfortable in this career. I felt capable of so much more and this knowledge was gnawing away at me. Everyone was full of advice and my team mates warned me not to take on the cycle challenge without the necessary training. In effect, in my mind I connected this advice to my future career. I was planning to attend many courses and, throughout my life, I had been hard at work in the rough and tumble of practical training. There was so much more ahead for me to learn—and I was aware of it. The painful muscles in the cycle race related to the career change challenge.

Note too, how critical and timely that call was from my team mate the very moment I was about to give up on the race. His encouraging words alone helped to change my thoughts and my mind. The guilt I felt when I found my boss's wife waiting for me at the finish line was also significant. There was guilt when I wanted to give up halfway, and there was added guilt when she met me and congratulated me on finishing.

Chapter 16 - Energy Guidance

(Approximate age 34, year 2002)

It is Saturday morning and I am preparing for the arrival of a meditation group. Today I am to do the teaching. For the first time, I have chosen to do a healing protection around our house and yard, just outside the border of our gate and walls. I want to implement the new techniques I have learned in my Reiki healing degree. I am feeling rather apprehensive and sit in silence to do my own meditation and healing protection on myself, in preparation for the group. However, having done the meditation, I still feel uncomfortable. I decide to repeat the protection process on myself again. Now I am feeling much calmer and more confident. The phone starts ringing and one after another, members of the group call to say they will not be able to make it today. I have to accept it, but can't help wondering why this is happening. I even think of cancelling, as only two will now be coming. I realise that it is too late as they would probably be on their way. I go outside with keys and remote in hand, to allow cars in. Within minutes my friend, Stacey, arrives with her husband in his small truck. I wonder if he is going to join in too or whether he is just dropping her off. I walk to the small gate where they have stopped. I am about to open the gate; Stacey is climbing out of the car and saying good-bye to her husband and young daughter. Out of the blue, another car pulls up, brakes screeching. I first think this must be the other woman who is joining our group, but it is not. The driver slams on brakes and screeches to a halt in the middle of the road with the sole purpose of blocking the road. A man jumps and runs from the passenger side towards Stacey's husband. I hear him cock a gun. I am completely aware of what is going on. I still feel rather calm, though, and my only fear is that he will pull that trigger. I mentally proceed to place an energy block around her husband and child and in front of the barrel of the gun, with the intention of sending the bullet off course. Fortunately, Stacey's husband reacts fast and, with the engine still running, shifts gear and reverses down the road to safety. The gun is now pointed at Stacey, sending terror through her. I again place energy protection around her with the intention of pulling her closer to the gate, into the protected area I have pre-set around the property. A second man, armed with a knife, runs from the car towards her. Stacey gives this man her handbag in negotiation for her life. She takes a step towards the gate as the gunman shouts at me to open it. I refuse. Stacey comes closer to the gate and the first man is insisting I open it. I refuse once more. He shifts the gun back and forth, from me, inside the gate, and at Stacey, on the other side. His hand sways from side to side, keeping us both covered. Miraculously, I am in complete awareness and control of my emotions and actions. I mentally confirm the protection I placed on the borders of my property earlier, and now affirm more protection in this crisis moment. I mentally place an energy block in front of the gun again as it beams into my face. I am holding the keys for the gate and am ready to open it as and when the moment arises. The hijacker with the gun tells me again to open the gate, but I hold open my hand saying, "I don't know which key it is," pretending I am too shattered to know which one is which. I know exactly which key will open the gate. I realise that they may resort to rape, now that they have missed out on gaining the car. I look this man directly in the eyes, attempting to control him with an energy block through my eyes. He is now really angry and nervous and tells us both to close our eyes and to lie face down on the ground. He forbids us to look at him. We both lie on the ground, but I try not to lose eye contact, trying to control his actions with my stare. Stacey, outside the gate, is terrified and I slowly reach my hand under the gate towards her. For a moment, I think this is the end for both of us. I pray softly, asking God for all the protection possible, and immediately feel the strong presence of my spirit guides. At that moment my daughter, Casey, and my mother, Colleen, come out of the house. They are totally unaware of what is happening. Casey sees the hijacker with the gun and screams. To protect my mom and daughter, I consciously send a stream of energy their way, to push them back into the house. They turn and run. Casey's scream has sent terror through this man and he starts shaking uncontrollably as he tries to hold the gun on us. I lost eye contact with him when I turned to my family and realise this is not good, as he could accidentally pull the trigger as his hand is shaking, out of control. I know I need to take more action. So I mentally place both men into a bubble of loving energy and keep repeating in my mind over and over, "Go now, go now, get in your car and go, go". The man with the knife tells his partner they should leave. They turn away, climb into the car and drive off. Now I let my protection of defence down and as shock rises I start to tremble. I am unable to insert the key into the keyhole in the gate as my hands are shaking uncontrollably. I press the remote and ask Stacey to come through the other gate. When she's inside the yard we are all shaking. We can't get through to the police there is an answering machine 'on duty'. I call the cell phone emergency number and finally get through. Our neighbour comes out of her house and has also been trying to get hold of the police, since she saw what was happening. We all go inside and lock the doors. Stacey is pregnant and I can sense that her baby is disturbed as she is in great shock. I sit her down, calm myself first, and then do a brief healing and calming on her. From the healing I know for certain that her unborn baby is under great stress. I use my discernment and don't tell her this as it would worry her further. I encourage her to have her baby checked-up on immediately.

Stacey's father arrives to fetch and support her. Her husband is too shocked and fearful to return to my house. The police arrive and we give all the details. Stacey is upset and angry with herself for giving her handbag to them. I become aware of her baby stressing again and try to calm her down by assuring her that she will get her bag back. I tell her that it was the natural thing to do to keep them from becoming violent. At least they think they have scored something for their efforts. I tell her that by giving them the bag, she may have saved us all from disaster. The police look at me as if to say, "Listen, naïve lady, there is less than no chance of getting her bag back," but they probably realise why I said it and say nothing further. At that very moment the police radio crackles and a report comes through that the very same vehicle was used a mere two blocks away in another hijacking, successfully this time. One policeman speeds off after the hijackers while the other stays behind to take our statements.

When everyone has left, I realise how calm I was throughout the ordeal and I know that it was because of the protection and guides that were present with me. The aftermath of the event has left me in a state of hyperactivity and I know that I have been running on pure adrenaline. In a highly restless state, I return to the position where it all took place and water the garden. I reflect on the events, at the scene, in order to heal myself quickly. I find myself imparting healing energies to the plants as they also experienced this event. Tears of relief flow and I long for a hug from my husband. He is unaware of the events and I can't contact him as he went out without his cell phone. I continue watering the garden, mentally pleading for my husband's presence. Dustin has called my sister-in-law, Jane, and she rushes over to give us her support. About half-an-hour later, my husband arrives. I feel so relieved and I just want him to hold me so that I can feel a little secure and safe. Casey and Dustin meet him at the gate and tell him what has happened. He walks up to me, keeps his distance, and angrily wants to know "What's this all about now?" He shakes his head, retraces his steps to his car and drives away. I have missed out on my hug. "How can he walk away?" I think. Two hours later he returns and this time I choose to ignore him. By lunchtime Stacey calls to say that the police have found her bag. Someone saw the expensive bag being thrown out of the window and contacted the police. Not all the contents are in it, but at least she has her credit and bank cards back. And finding the handbag gave the police a hint as to which direction the hijackers took.

At the end of the day, the other lady who was to attend the meeting never turned up. Another blessing was that Stacey chose to be dropped off rather than to come in her own car, or she might have lost that as well. Her beautiful and strong baby boy also managed to survive the trauma. The biggest blessing was that none of us was shot, stabbed or raped. We may never know if the hijackers were ever found, but the important thing is that we survived!

Self-Interpretation Of Energy Guidance

My Reiki training here is a blessing and my intuition is stronger. My intuition is guiding me in the manner in which to repeat my protection techniques. Guidance took place so perfectly with all the people concerned, and at such short notice.

My friend's husband experienced a repeat pattern of another hijacking. He was recovering from a terrible experience a couple of weeks prior.

I remained totally in the present moment and focused throughout this event, as this added to the power I had within me. I was completely confident that I was in control of this situation.

My daughter's scream (through fear), rattled the hijacker and triggered the same reaction in him. This clearly is evidence of how all of us pick up the silent energies vibrating between us, and how important it is to always think of guarding how we react to, or treat, others. Always focus on the way in which we would like to be treated.

I was very aware of having him think he was completely and utterly in control, in order to read his intentions. This is probably directly opposite to the norm. I was able to send him off with calm, loving energies as well. The reaction from him was therefore reciprocal; I attracted the same vibration. All the spiritual guidance played a very important role too. Having known and trusted in God and my guide's presence gave me the confidence that we would be safe.

My healing abilities are completely awakened within me at this time of my life, and helping Stacey and her baby was not only the natural thing for me to do, it was also a privilege. My psychic knowledge of the return of her handbag is also to be noted.

Naturally, the shock of the event took its toll on my human mind and body, and that was the reason for the tears afterwards.

At this point in my life I have grown and I am more consciously aware and able to accept what takes place in the invisible world around us. I am able to instantly know the blessings and lessons to come out of any event. The lessons I learn in the course of my life obviously give me more confidence in the power and energy of spiritual guidance. I never experienced any further anger towards the hijackers. The energy I used was *transforming* energy. I therefore didn't suppress any anger. I also didn't need to experience my husband's anger as it was not my reaction. It was his. Hence, he departed quickly with his own baggage of emotions. My longing for my husband to be with me clearly indicated the dependant-type of relationship we shared, and the distance between us was, evidently, growing.

Chapter 17 - Past Life

(Approximate age 34, year 2002)

I have often sat on my front veranda, watching many people drive past. Too many choose our driveway in which to turn around. Sometimes I become frustrated at the increase in traffic in our street, since a main adjoining street has been 'beautified' with speed bumps to slow traffic down. I have applied feng shui techniques to my garden, such as placing Dustin's bird feeder strategically to enhance and boost my work-from-home business and to bring many helpful people. I know this is the one reason why many choose our driveway in which to turn around. Why have so many people lost their bearings and need to turn around? To transform the frustration and make good use of these many lost visitors, I decide to put up a sign for my business.

I have recently received my Reiki Master's degree attunements and I am following a body balancing and detox-eating programme. I have noticed a detox taking place on all levels of my being, not just the physical. I attempt to make myself a sign, from yellow plastic board. I create the lettering on the computer so that I can print it and then stick it on. To my dismay, this doesn't work too well. The letters bubble from the glue, the plastic board is transparent and I can't make the two-sided sign I have in mind. I give up and decide instead to have it made professionally. I realise I cannot afford the sign I want right now and feel frustrated, defeated, annoyed and angry at my finances. Days pass and once again I become inspired to attempt this sign again, this time with a wooden board and paint. I walk around my garage to discover that I have everything I need to complete the task without incurring any extra cost. I go ahead and paint a piece of wood with sealant, followed by pale yellow paint. I reprint the lettering from the computer and carbon the letters onto the yellow background. With this complete, I place the board on my healing bed which is the perfect height to accomplish the painting I want to do. I gather my tools: black paint, small jar of water and a thin paintbrush. As I touch the paintbrush, I recall how I used to paint with this brush as a small child. I had kept this particular light wooden paintbrush all these years. I grin to myself at how fortunate that was. I shake the small bottle of paint, open the lid and dip the tip of the paintbrush. I start painting the word 'Reiki' in Japanese writing. I feel so comfortable doing this and have the strange déjà vu feeling that I have painted letters in Japanese before. The black paint is so familiar and the movement of the strokes is quite natural to me. Although I am completely absorbed in the moment, I am aware of a sadness creeping over me from somewhere within. I turn around to put on some meditation music to help me relax further. I touch a screen that I recently made. It is comprised of pine-coloured wooden strips in squares and is covered with off-white, plastic-coated material. As I touch it, a clear vision flashes through my mind.

I am sitting on the floor next to a screen just like this one.

I restart my music and return to my task with paintbrush in hand.

As I start to paint, I see myself as a young Japanese/Chinese girl, possibly about five years old. I have a short-black, Oriental hairstyle and I'm wearing a cream linen dress. I am sitting on a bamboo rug on the floor with my back to the screen (just as I was standing at this moment with my back to my screen), *paper on the floor, a thin paintbrush in hand and black ink. I am feeling very sad and alone and have tears in my eyes. I am writing a letter in Japanese and find that I am able to translate this directly into English.*

"Dear daddy, why did you have to leave last night? Why did you not say goodbye to me? Why did you have to go back to your home in China? Why

105

didn't you stay with mommy and me? When will you come back? I feel that you won't be coming back. Do you love us still? Why did you leave in the night? Why didn't you take us with you? Are you scared of something? You could have held my hand, and I would have helped you to not be scared anymore, just like you always hold my hand when I am afraid. Daddy, will you write back to me if you can't come back soon? I want you to come back and teach me to be brave and calm and peaceful like you. How are you able to be like that Daddy? Why didn't you say goodbye and why didn't you wake me up? Why didn't you tell me you were leaving when I sat on your lap last night? Last night when you held me so tight in your hug, when you whispered in my ear, "I will always be with you," and you put your hand on my body, touching my heart so close. I woke up this morning running to see you. You were not there and mommy was sitting crying. Mommy held me close just like you did, but mommy was very sad. It made me sad too. Then she told me you needed to go away to your real home, for the work you needed to do. She prayed that one day we would all be together again. Mommy has been sitting, silently meditating and praying all day, Daddy. I've been crying with mommy too. I miss you already, Daddy. Please come home to us. Love, your little baby star, Nikkita. Beside me on the floor was an old photo of my daddy.

I had become so drawn into this vision and it felt so real. I had lost consciousness of time and space. I had already completed my Reiki words in Japanese without being aware of doing it. I was 'somewhere else,' while being moved to tears from this vision, reading my own letter, the lonely feeling still deep within. I shook my head to try to make sense of where I was and what I was doing. I went on to enjoy painting my sign to completion. I am aware of what really took place, and the healing that was arising within my Soul from a previous lifetime. This was all a part of my detox. I kept thinking how familiar the photo of my dad had looked to me. I knew him from somewhere else. Unable to put it all together right now, I let it go.

It is time to collect my children from school. We arrive home and I make lunch. I am absorbed in what my children are both urgently trying to tell me about their day–both at the same time. I reach into the cupboard and choose some noodles for lunch. We sit eating the noodles out of small pudding bowls. Again I have an instant memory, a vision so clear.

I'm sitting on the floor, the same night after I had written my letter to my daddy, eating noodles out of a small oriental bowl with chopsticks in my right hand. Sadness is still with me as my daddy is not eating with us.

I return to my current reality and silently eat my noodles with my fork. For the remainder of the day I find myself pondering what I saw and what went through my mind. I find myself putting together the pieces of a puzzle I have often wondered about. I have gathered many feng shui and Chinese ornaments as well as Japanese pictures. I have an intense interest in feng shui and I find that I am always drawn to Zen gardens.

One of my wedding presents, from Jane and Trevor, now starts making sense. It was a bronze plaque portraying a Japanese landscape and people, and Japanese writing all around it. My husband also brought home many gifts and photos from his trips to Japan. They all seem to be telling me that I have been there before. I have an intense longing to visit the country. When I look at certain pictures I have the distinct feeling I have been there before. In my corporate world career, I was called upon to arrange two Chinese functions. I had also gathered Chinese decorations through the years. My son had a Chinese project to do for school, and in true "mother-will-help" style, I got involved and enjoyed it immensely. I also have several sets of chopsticks lying around the house, although I can't recall where they came from.

Today, I am able to piece all of this together; I know why my daddy's photo in this vision is so familiar; he is the spirit guide who is still with me, guiding me and teaching me. He was once my father, in another lifetime.

Self-Interpretation Of Past Life

Here again, this is indicative of how my own healing is powerfully in action and shifting my consciousness into awareness. I am cleansing out 'past' lives, which have been carried forward into my present existence. I am in the process of awakening to more of my mystic self.

Notice how current actions and objects are triggers to bring memories of my past existence from my subconscious to my conscious. It was extremely significant that I chose my healing bed for this painting task and not my desk. The pre-set healing energies on my healing bed obviously have a powerful influence on my healing activities. I had not realised at the time that there was still much healing ahead of me.

That letter I was writing in another life clearly shows that my father must have abandoned my mother and me for some reason. Or perhaps he died. My writing abilities are evident, too, from a past-life, and deeply ingrained in my Soul. This also explains the feeling of abandonment in chapter 1; and my astral healing dream in this lifetime, where I connect it with the time when my own father, in this lifetime, was in the army. This shows how energies such as fears and emotions in ones' life usually are carried forward, to be dealt with again when we re-incarnate, to bring healing full circle. This all proves to me that healing should not be viewed in terms of one existence in one lifetime only, but on a whole Soul level through many lives.

My request in another existence when I said, "I want you to come back and teach me to be brave like you, calm and peaceful like you" has been granted—in another era and in another place. My past father, now one of my spirit guides, is teaching and guiding me in meditation and feng shui. Here lies the origin of the calmness and peace I now choose to live in, because meditation has always been a natural technique for the Chinese and Japanese.

Chapter 18 - This Book

(Age 35, year 2003)

I repeatedly acknowledge my many thoughts to write a book. My self-doubts attempt to distract me.

"I am not a writer and I have no topic to write about."

I push the thoughts from my mind in an effort to keep myself positively in-tune. I feel the strong flow of words about my past running through my mind. I tell myself I need to write this down, to release my past from my head; that it will be a good healing technique for me, and of course, I love healing. I admit to myself that if I were to do that, I would end up with a book, as there are many past events to record. Again, I push the thoughts away and continue with my present life. I am well within conscious transformation, busy with my Reiki Master degree.

I am also attending a communication course titled "Let's Talk". I feel a great need to be present on this course, not really knowing why, other than to benefit my practical skills of communicating with clients. The lectures are resonating with me, twanging chords that I was only subconsciously aware of before; however, I am aware of something significant. I am not a woman of many verbal words, perhaps that's the reason I'm on this course, I tell myself, or perhaps there are other reasons. Fellow students comment on how silent I appear to be. I never talk. However, I am fully aware that the level of my communication is on a different one to theirs. I was truly awakened to my level at our first lecture. I have been communicating loudly, strongly and powerfully. I sit and listen to the conversations being exchanged, I resonate and acknowledge loudly within, the words I want to say. As I am about to put up my hand, too late, one of my fellow students speaks my words, as if they were directly in my mind and thoughts. I allow myself to enjoy "listening" to my own words being spoken from someone else. "Good team-work," I announce to myself. I recognise how much fun this communication is; nevertheless, they appear to be unaware of how I am communicating.

I often write letters to the universe, with words that resonate with my silent inner voice, often burning the letters as a release technique. I wonder which form of communication is really the more powerful. We all assume it is the verbal voice. The more I ponder this, the more aware I become of how written words out-live the verbal voice, out-live the human lifetime. I observe in this course, and in my Reiki Master degree, how many people turn to books for help, answers, guidance: everyone is reading. The Bible is a perfect example of how far-reaching the written word is. "How many lives has the Bible touched? How many lives has the Bible out-lived?"

This particular morning I awake with a sense of uncertainty. I ask God for guidance in finding answers to this feeling I have acknowledged within. "If there is more I need to accomplish in this life, which I am currently unaware of, please give me a clear sign."

I arrive at my lecture. In past lectures I sat in a different seat each week. This lecture I choose to sit on the end, in the back row. The lecture starts in an unexpected way, unlike all the previous ones. Our lecturer announces he wants to share with us something which is unrelated to our course. He has just published his own financial book, and now proudly shares his accomplishment with us. He passes his book around. Everyone is admiring it, and I wonder to myself, what is the reason he is sharing his book with us today? I feel connected to his book. Perhaps it is the finance subject. I spent a number of years in the corporate world as a financial secretary. However, this doesn't fit comfortably with me. Eventually, his book lands in my hands. "Wow!" As I touch it, I hear the words in my mind, "This is your sign." I have a deep, overpowering feeling of just knowing this is my sign, the one I had asked for. I become so involved in my present feelings, totally disconnected from the lecture. I sit touching the cover, trying to focus on reading the back cover; I am completely absorbed in my feelings. The words I read don't penetrate. I flip through the pages, sensing I no longer resonate with finance. I feel my *own book* rising to the surface of my consciousness. My chords are twanging loud and strong. With no one next to me to pass his book on, I remain seated with his book in my hands, vibrating almost too loudly to my own tune.

I realise I now need to move my focus off his book to his lecture; I need to absorb his teachings. I find it really difficult this day. I hear my own silent voice acknowledging this sign, giving thanks, in this moment. I now know for certain, I need to write my own book. I remain unaware of my theme for the book. I recall a book I read in my early stages of learning hands-on healing. 'The Journey' by Brandon Bays, captured my true essence. I was encouraged by her book and continued, inspired, to document my own journey.

Tea break arrives and I finally part with the book in my hands. I am now able to focus on the present.

Days gallop by, the thought of writing a book leaps from my subconscious into my conscious, twanging harder and stronger and demanding my full attention. I associate signs I continue to attract all around me.

On the TV, people writing books; I read about people writing books; I hear people around me wanting to write a book; all signs ensuring I receive the message loud and clear. I have gathered books all around me, from which I learn, and allow to guide me on my healing journey. I wonder for what reason I have just entered into a fruitless 'work-from-home' typing venture. I am 'typing up' books for other people. One book is about sewing. My eyes and fingers remain connected in the rhythm of typing; my mind disconnected in self-communication. "What is the purpose of this?" I was once passionate about sewing but had quickly outgrown it. My mind is now drifting around in search of answers. I am becoming more aware of my own passion lying very deep within. I know I love typing, the only talent I wish to continue from my corporate world. I am further awakened to whose book I could be typing. I end my typing venture writing others' stories, to do my own.

I remember myself as a young girl before school days, sitting with a pen and small book, writing squiggles that only I could comprehend. I could spend an entire day writing my own words; completely absorbed in my own present little world. I always called my squiggles 'Chinese writing'. Rather odd for a child who hadn't attended school yet, having never been taught that China or Chinese writing existed. I now completely allow myself to accept that writing a book is what I need to do, but I am still unsure of the theme.

My day arrives to receive the last of my Reiki Master attunements, earlier than I had expected. I spend the day after my attunements in a blissful, silent, humble peace; complete serenity that I have never felt before. A miraculous feeling, sent straight from God, is Soul-integration into my physical being. I wonder to myself if this is a short-lived feeling, or whether I will feel like this for the rest of my life, through all of life's ups and downs.

On awaking the next morning I am immediately aware that this feeling of serenity remains somewhere deep within me, a place untouchable by life's knocks. I continue to consciously awaken. I have a strong sense of something that I need to be doing. I feel a disturbance within, as I am not sure what it really is. The day moves on, the feeling growing. I rest my body late that night, thankful and grateful for this wonderful serenity, and questioning this disturbance swirling around inside. I fall asleep.

I awake the next morning, leap out of bed and rush through my daily chores as excitement vibrates, too strong to contain. I announce to my husband "I am going to write a book. I am going to write it NOW. I know the topic. I know the contents." He looks at me strangely, possibly thinking, "What happened to her last night?" He lets me be. I sit down at my computer, my fingers dancing merrily across the keyboard at a speed the computer is having difficulty translating. My written text, word for word, flows powerfully through my mind, my body and my fingers, in the same manner universal life-force energy flows. I'm out of control, I'm so happy; I'm so peaceful and content. Time races ahead of me as I sit from 08:00 am to 08:00 pm totally absorbed by my flow of the written word, captivated by my new direction. The next day I wake at 3:00 am unable to sleep, my words flowing hard and strong, like a huge waterfall, through my mind. By 4:30 am I really have to get out of bed, I am unable to settle, my body is vibrating with a huge urgency to leap upon my computer. I need to put my words to paper, there are too many for my mind to handle.

I'm feeling a different sensation coming from my body today; I convince myself it is only from lack of sleep and the urgent words tumbling out of me. I sit alone in the dark, looking at my brightly lit computer screen, again totally absorbed as I capture my past memories into my present. 07:00 am arrives; my husband wakes and brings me a cup of tea. I accept his gesture as a need to take a break.

I rise from my chair with a sudden and sharp stabbing pain piercing my lower right abdomen and absorbing all my attention. I place my hands directly on the painful area, the most natural thing to do. I move as if carrying myself, one step at a time. I ask this pain what it is. I hear ovarian cyst ringing loud and clear in my thoughts. I know it is true, but wonder why I had not picked this up before, through all my own self-healing. As I question, I hear amidst my thoughts, "This is divine timing". I accept and acknowledge an ovarian cyst. I retrace my written words moments before the pain shook through me.

I was writing about the hysterectomy that was helping me release and heal. I happened to have stopped writing at a critical point, where successful healing did not take place in my life. I had suppressed the need for healing in that moment so many years ago. I am completely aware this cyst may have been silently developing through all these years. I am unable to sit and type my words now. The words that are flowing in my mind now appear not to match my previous words. I am stuck. I think this must be what is called 'writer's block', or 'healer's block', my choice of words twanging more of my own chords. I have a blockage in my ovary; in my life, that now needs to be cleared. I know healing must take place. Choosing not to do this alone, I phone my friend, a fellow Reiki Master, and ask if she would share her healing touch with me today.

When I lie on her healing bed I tell her, "I have an ovarian cyst we need to heal". I close my eyes to relax as she prepares herself for healing. I hear my spirit guide, "*Japanese doctor*", speaking telepathically, with divine-loving energy radiating out towards me. "You do have a cyst, but you will need to have a scan. You and your doctor need to see the scan."

I reply, "If you confirm there is a cyst then there is no need to see a scan, the need is only healing." He replies with urgency in his tone, "You must release what is concealed within this cyst or it will become cancerous. You must go for a scan tomorrow."

I acknowledge his communication and confirm I will allow myself to heal, in whatever way is necessary and with a scan.

During the healing session, my release starts of feelings that have been long and deeply imbedded in my subconscious that I chose to run from, to hide from, to bury further, not ever really understanding where suppressed thoughts and feelings settle. I did what many do, unaware of the outcome that it has on our physical body at a later stage.

For the first time, I totally accept and forgive past events, thoughts and feelings. And with amazing speed, I feel a major shift taking place within me.

The following morning I wonder if I really need to go for the scan. Each time I receive a reply directly from my guide. He is listening to my thoughts. Is he sitting on my shoulder?

"You and your doctor need to see the scan; he will also teach you more about your body." He is right, only the scan will give me absolute proof that I have a cyst. Finally I go to my doctor's rooms yet again: a place I had visited far too often, a place I had been running from, not wanting to ever return to. But, here I am, once again. I impatiently ask my doctor to take a look at my right ovary as I think I have a cyst. He proceeds to examine the point of pain; he suggests I have a quick scan.

To my surprise, my doctor has taken a course to carry out his own scans, so there's no need for a tedious trip to the radiologists. He proceeds, having fun with his new-found talents, with the opportunity to show me all my organs, like a child with a new toy. He shows me I am still alive: my heart is beating. "There is your heart," he explains. I am so fascinated, no radiologist has ever been interested enough to take the time to point out my body parts! He was certainly teaching me more. On the screen appears a very big cyst on my right ovary, too big to be real, too big to have been without pain until yesterday. I catch my breath, this is real.

My doctor exclaims, "Don't you believe me? It is real, Tina." I wondered if he knew he has just used words that match my thoughts. "This may have been building up since your hysterectomy," he explains. I start feeling a little down and disappointed, "Why?" I ask my guides silently. I hear the words, "This is your blessing."

I rise from the bed, filled with confidence again for the healing process that is ahead. I go back to his room and, face to face, hear the words I've heard too often. "You now need to get this removed." Inside I feel my entire body saying, "No". I ask if the cyst alone can be removed and not the ovary. "Yes, it can, but really, Tina, how often do you use your ovary?" He laughs with his great sense of humour, changing the energy in the environment, lifting my spirits again, just what I needed. I laugh too and suddenly reply unexpectedly.

"Well," I say, "You are passing those words through the mind of a Reiki Master, and I want to explain how important this ovary is to me." He is captivated by my words; he stops writing my referral letter to a gynaecologist and meets my direct eye contact.

I continue, "This ovary is a representation of my point of creativity, which I am currently using to write a book about my own conscious healing moments. I need this ovary and, in fact, I need this cyst to help me through some healing right now. It all ties in with my hysterectomy.

"Let's rather leave it. I know it will heal."

"You must come back in three weeks then, for a check-up" he firmly points out. I agree. I leave feeling blessed, through illness for the first time in my life. I am no longer filled with anger and guilt-ridden, as I had been so many times before. I am truly thankful. I wonder if anyone else has ever been able to be thankful when something goes wrong in his or her body. I know a lot of healing and releasing work still awaits me. I know, too, that true blessings are still to come from this cyst.

I remember the words from our deputy dean, in our last Reiki lecture on anger: "The month ahead may be a difficult one." I now understand what kind of release this is going to involve: my suppressed anger towards men, the reason the cyst is attached to my right ovary and not my left. I am unable to go back to writing my book right now. I allow myself the time to focus on my body.

I read and study further, discovering I have been 'an anger avoider and suppressor'. My moment arrives and emotions surge, tears overflow and hurt and anger seethe, I allow them all out. I welcome this, despite having a difficult day as I express my anger, alone in my home.

I decide to visit a special chapel that brings me tremendous peace and focus. I am tempted to give up writing my book. I phone my friend to see if she wants to join me at the chapel. She says no and I feel relieved; I do need to be alone.

She stops my thoughts and announces, "About your book you started and let me read-I want to urge you to carry on with it; you really must carry on." I am shocked yet encouraged by her words to keep me on track, knowing how in-tune we are in thought. Well-connected and following her own intuition, she knew what I was thinking just before I called. I understand what an amazing inspiration she is to me at this time, and what a blessing.

116

I allowed her to read my very first unedited words as they were important steps in my healing process and I had chosen her to help me with this healing.

As days pass, I observe many people interacting in the natural emotion of anger. I allow myself to feel more comfortable as I watch their emotions unfold. I am aware of which my anger is; and which belongs to others. I no longer allow myself to become involved in their anger, instead focusing and acknowledging my own.

Healing progresses and I begin dancing to music I love, gliding, almost floating to the vibration, feeling like I am in my same world with new eyes, a new mind and a new vibration. I sing as I move, like never before. I look at myself in my large framed mirror, observing the difference in my reflection. I look like a graceful swan.

"I am happy, I am blessed," the words stumble out of me, in a tune I know. A song leaps from my subconscious, the jingle of cell phone advert on TV, 'A happy communication'. Casey and Dustin drove my husband and me crazy singing this song continually, just recently on our holiday. We couldn't stop them so we joined in and learnt the words. I find myself singing along with the tune, changing some of the words to fit my current bodily needs, and avoiding some negative words too.

"I'm happy, I'm feeling glad, I have sunshine in my ovary, I have sunshine in my body, and the future is coming on, coming on." Dustin hears the song he took part in teaching and programming into his mother's mind, both of us unaware it would prove inspiring in this healing task that was ahead for me. He notices I'm singing it 'wrong'.

"No, mommy, it goes like this, 'I'm happy, I'm feeling glad, I've got sunshine in a bag, I'm useless, but not for long, the future is coming on, coming on". I allow him to sing his own song, with a smile on my face, thankful for his teachings.

I discover I am able to bounce back into action on the keyboard, continuing with my writing. I have a sense of urgency about helping many people around the world heal themselves through my book. I know my book will outlive my lifetime and will reach out to all who are unable to hear my silent voice. I now know I am at this communication course to learn a new way of communication; one that will help to build a bridge for my silent voice to cross. I accept my gift to become an inspiring guide through communication. *Be Aware*. "When all is silent you may just hear my voice."

The next time you choose to listen to your thoughts, stop and ask, "Is this my own thought or is it from someone else?" Now, if I have just twanged one of your chords, *listen* carefully, and ask yourself, "What am I going to do with my tune, awakened from my own subconscious?"

I return three weeks later for my scan check-up with my doctor, a mixture of confidence and anxiety swirling in my stomach. The cold lubricating gel connects the electronic eyes to my body. My doctor quietly confirms the cyst has reduced by more than half its size. Wow! Gratitude sweeps its way through my entire body, my encouragement to continue healing vibrating strongly. I silently thank all my guides for their help. My doctor gives me another four weeks before another check-up. I leave with satisfaction, in light strides to my car.

I continue with all my healing processes as before, meditating and practicing Reiki daily. I take myself back into my book to stimulate my healing. My emotions shift strongly as I record and recall many past angry moments in my life, and I connect their presence to important awakenings I had chosen to experience.

Two weeks later I am satisfied the cyst has completely dissolved. I choose to visit my doctor earlier than scheduled. Lying confidently on the bed, my doctor shares his talented skill with a view into my body. We are both pleased to see a perfect ovary, with no trace of a cyst. An even greater gratitude engulfs me, a realisation of what I have truly accomplished.

My doctor once again guides me through all my internal organs. I am pleased I have a doctor who takes the time to show and teach me more of what I need to learn; validating my internal views, matching all my past visualisations.

Self-Interpretation Of This Book

At times I still allow my own negative self-doubt to interfere with my life here and do not always trust myself. However, I am far more aware at this time in my life and powerfully trust my spirituality.

Guidance is clearly coming forward to me through people and TV. I am thankfully aware of these signs as guidance.

It is interesting to note that within the communication course we learnt how to communicate more with our bodies by asking our bodies or organs what the problem is. This you can see me doing when the ovarian cyst appeared.

You can now see the effects of positive healing that have lifted me into a higher and lighter vibration of energy, hence the dancing and singing.

Chapter 19 - Communication

(Approximate age 35, year 2003)

I decide it is time to investigate the reasons why I suppress most of my verbal communications, which appears to annoy many people more than it does me. I know it is going to involve some powerful healing on my throat chakra, the chakra of communication.

I relax on my healing bed, my hot vibrating hands gently cradling my throat, my eyes closed. I feel the universal energies vibrating out of my hands into my throat; I follow the energies and visualise blue energy penetrating deep into my cells. Moments later a flood of memories surface from my subconscious and with it, unexpected emotions attached to the memories. I recall my childhood sexual abuse experience and the words attached to the scene to ensure I don't tell anyone about this, as no-one will ever believe me. I remember many people telling me to 'shut-up' as I talk too much. I allow myself to cry, just as the small child I was should have cried years ago. I allow the emotional and mental release to take place. I drift into a meditative state and complete peace soothes my body. Sometime later I lift out of meditation and check on my healing. There are no more tears or emotions or negative thoughts connected to the memories. I know my healing has taken place. I now need to re-programme my mind in positive ways. I sit up and imagine myself talking to people and feeling confident as others hear my healed voice. I also begin to enjoy hearing my own voice speaking aloud. Every day I practise choosing to speak my internal thoughts out loud, empowering them with confidence and love. My voice now carries the power that was for so long suppressed. People begin to comment on how different my voice sounds. They tell me it has lost its squeaking, childish pitch. I am so inspired when I hear this because I know my self-healing was again a success. I realise how my voice was stuck in a childhood tone, at the age my blockage was created. I record my voice on tape, and compare it to previous recordings I had made before this healing. I, too, hear a definite change in my tone. I acknowledge with satisfaction that if it hadn't been for this blockage, I may never have begun my writing journey.

Self-Interpretation Of Communication

This is an indication of Reiki hands-on healing. As you apply the energy to your body, it is absorbed. All the information required to begin the releasing process is recorded within your cells. Then up comes what lies within and, in my case, what was causing the blockage.

My blockage was words that were imprinted on my mind at a most traumatic time. Through the years, I had absorbed more and more negative words that programmed me further to believe I should 'shut-up'. I suppressed the words I wanted to say, without realising the accumulation of energy was creating damage within my physical body. I found it astounding that others immediately noticed the change in the tone of my voice, a true indication of a healing success.

Chapter 20 - Clearing Patterns

(Approximate age 35, year 2003)

I attend another course, one of many since I left the corporate world. I'm well aware of the studies I need to undertake for my new career. I want to perfect my ability to communicate with my spirit guides, for the clear help and guidance they give me. I recognise how in-tune I already am with them and that it is only self-doubt that stands in my way. I receive an explanation for the very recent information that was withheld from me by my spirit guides. I now completely understand why, at other times in my life, information was withheld. I am given the advice I want on the direction in which my future lies and the work ahead of me in writing books. I learn how our guides are always in communication with us. Often through TV, music, thoughts, other people, books-in fact anywhere that we are prepared to notice. I have the thought it would be a great feeling to donate blood someday to help someone, as I have never done this before. I reach down to pick up our local newspaper, which falls open as I lift it off the floor. I see a picture of the newly opened local blood bank. Drawn into this, I read the article and know I need to go there. Later, I sit in front of the TV, which is completely out of my routine. My husband flips through TV channels with the remote and skips past the news. I stop him and insist he return to the news. I never take time to watch the news because of the negativity the media often brings to our attention. But I am captivated by the story I am hearing and watching.

A 16-year-old girl is in desperate need of a bone marrow donor for leukaemia treatment. My attention is caught as her surname is the name of the street I live in. Her sister, Tina, in explaining the situation further, mentions that the procedure will involve her ovary. I was still in the process of healing my own ovarian cyst. Hearing my own name on TV, I know there is a message here for me. A woman from the bone marrow association comes on-screen, also with the name Tina. Goodness me, two women named Tina in one shot! I am completely shaken to awareness. The next day I take myself off to the blood bank, to provide a sample of blood in the hope I may be a match, although the chances are slim.

Weeks later I stumble on the news that a donor had been found for her. I am not the one to help her. I wonder whether there is a connection to my traumatic experience of a leukaemia test when I had bilharzia. I note that further healing needs to take place to release the trauma associated with all the various medical tests to establish the bilharzia diagnosis. I am aware that this is a typical warning sign, to clear my patterns.

Self-Interpretation Of Clearing Patterns

I take time to release the trauma associated with the finding of my having had bilharzia and the connection to leukaemia.

Through a hands-on healing that travels deep into the cells in my blood, I connect my thoughts of "What's the use?" to how I have withheld a deep secret from my parents all these years. It has been eating away at me, especially whenever sexual abuse was mentioned. I now have a sense of that it has become irrelevant since it happened so many years ago-and I have already accomplished my own healing. But knowing that a secret, deeply withheld over a long period, can lead to the development of cancer cells, I accept this as a warning for an effective prevention exercise. I must tell my parents as soon as possible. Without prevention and/or awareness, leukaemia could be the next illness to speak out for attention. Fortunately, I acknowledge this guidance as prevention. I am also confident that if I am too late to prevent any form of cancer cells, I will be successful in healing it.

Chapter 21 – Face The Truth

(Approximate age 35, year 2003)

A cold winter evening in June 2003 is shattered with feverish heat as my body begins responding to something unknown. Nausea rises and subsides with waves of intensity, pains squeeze my colon and diarrhoea begins. Fear vibrates through my body very strongly. What is happening? I ask myself. I surrender into the night feeling very ill and without answers, other than knowing something is about to happen.

I think to myself, "This is my final release to sexual abuse" and I announce this to my husband. I succeed through the night in total surrender to illness and give my body time to rest the next day.

When evening arrives, my answers to the fear and illness stand before my eyes.

I open the door and come face to face with my childhood abuser. He has flown across the world to meet with me and discuss the events of the sexual abuse in my childhood. I run off to my room alone, in terror and tears, with a 'what now' feeling.

My husband joins me and holds me in his tight and loving embrace, offering comfort and security and, convincing me it is all right. He has been the only one who has known, since meeting me, that I was abused and who my sexual abuser was.

I spend the night distant and in my own world, completing preparations for what is ahead for the week. I somehow manage to sleep peacefully. Waking with full strength and courage, I manage to avoid any private union with this man for the day. The following day dawns too quickly, but I feel the strength and courage that is operating in full force and know that this will carry me through the ordeal.

Finally I sit, courageously, face to face with him. For the first time since my childhood we have an open discussion about the events of the abuse. This is both my moment and his, for each of us to view our positions as victim and victimiser, in open communication.

I feel gratitude bubbling within me. I am now able to sit with him, in total, unconditional love and forgiveness. I know how much deep work I have truly accomplished to arrive at this point. Not all easy, but successful!

A powerful thought consumes my mind how important forgiveness and acceptance truly is! What it must take for a Soul such as his to choose to engage in, to commit, some of the worst crimes and karmic creations. And to experience the values and strengths this brings out in another Soul, such as I. This is where we need to feel and know the importance of, and gratitude for, what others do, both for and to us, to assist our progression in spiritual growth. Yes, I do believe, even those terrible, criminal acts.

I sit in compassion as he expresses his side of the events, his own 'sentence' that he served in the prison of his long-withheld guilt and anguish, one that had trapped him in both his mind and his life.

We end the conversation with me giving him a Reiki healing treatment. I feel an increase in my energies as I shift into a deeper level of unconditional love, without any personal attachment to this man or the sexual abuse, my own test passed, with abounding success.

We continue to enjoy the week together in a relationship healed into another level of existence.

Some months later I take a bold step towards setting my health straight. I tell my parents the shocking news: the secret I kept of sexual abuse in my childhood. The powerful feeling of freedom in releasing a 30-year-old secret that I have kept from them and, that is now in the open, feels wonderful. An incredible lightness fills me. I wonder how many people take secrets to their deathbeds without realising that they could have freed themselves of many illnesses by just coming out into the open with the truth. I am sure few people know that they are causing themselves some of the most uncomfortable and, often, incurable illnesses by doing this, without connecting the mind and emotions to the physical body.

This is where I want to help you!

Self-Interpretation Of Face The Truth

See how my body is tuned into the subconscious and my psychic abilities guide the way without my conscious knowing. At the same time this man climbed on a plane to fly across the world, I was in connection with what was taking place. My body was responding, talking to me. My preparation and an unconscious down-loading, probably of the thoughts he too was going through on his journey on the plane, his own preparations of words to say to me, and how to react; his own shifting and healing being guided for his own growth directly in accordance with his Soul. From far across the world we were connected for healing purposes. We are all connected!

Chapter 22 – Metaphysical Fun

(Approximate age 35, year 2003)

I am awake at 3:45 am, unable to sleep with a hyperactive mind gaining awareness on my life. This energy needs to be removed before I can expect to sleep. But then again, if one is physically awake and consciously awake, what is the point of going back to sleep? Why not enjoy writing what needs to be written, with a whole lot of healing fun? This is what I call 'acceptance of useful insomnia'.

I do already trust that tomorrow will take care of itself, but I definitely am guilty of needing to release many days' accumulation of processing the new awareness in my life. The absorption of higher, positive, dimensional energies is causing my insomnia; too many words, thoughts, feelings and understandings were guiding me to write.

I am gaining a different awareness from recent events, guided through my daughter, Casey and the care required for her earlier diagnosed ADD (Attention Deficit Dis-order). I have been calmed, relieved and excited as therapy progresses, which is sure to give us positive results soon. However, just as I am seeing the light, the so-called 'darkness' re-surfaces. My daughter refuses to attend her next appointment, explaining to me that I am not respecting her as she does not want to go to the psychologist.

Our newly appointed psychologist confirmed the previous diagnosis of ADD, and now confirmed her having ODD (Oppositional Defiant Dis-order), two labelled problems, not one. I now know from my own experiences that problems are truly blessings. So this could mean Casey has come to earth with two unique blessings with which she may possibly assist in changing society as it is. With her amazingly strong ability to oppose some of the order many of us just accept and conform to, she has the ability to create peace by acknowledging that change ahead is necessary.

Being as aware as I am, I am grateful I have the ability to see some of these blessings concealed within the two dis-orders.

I analyse myself with the help of Doreen Virtue's book, "The Care and Feeding of Indigo Children". 'Indigo' is a relatively new term for children with particular traits that include ADD and ADHD (Attention Deficit Hyperactivity Disorder). I discover that I also fit with the description of an indigo child/parent. I must therefore be the perfect super-different mother Casey needs. Doreen Virtue points to a positive direction in her labelling of ADHD as "Attention Dialled into a Higher Dimension". Now that so accurately fits me.

I awaken the healing psychologist within me and take a good look at my own mind. I could quite easily label myself with some psychological dis-orders. This could result in negatively running me down rather than positively tuning me up.

How do people manage to boost themselves up when a label is stuck on them to point them down again? Now my mind expands, dialling into the higher dimension. Who created this labelling, these words, that describe illness and dis-orders? Who created the dictionary? It is another book to touch many lives. Obviously a super-different human created the words. Well, many believe God created everything. So, if God created the Bible, then the dictionary may be another form of a bible that he created too. Did you ever think this? If God is already within us we are then ALL super-different humans. I have now begun analysing my mind. You may understand now why I have insomnia, I probably would be having nightmares if I were sleeping, but thankfully I am **awake.**

However, analysing isn't what we should be doing, as this leads to judging, so I will change the label to a description of playful fun within my mind. I welcome you all to play along with me.

Now, firstly, I ask you, "Where is your mind?" Well, I can't say where anyone else's mind is, but I know my own is everywhere, inside of me and outside of me. My mind is then consciousness. I find it is time to consult the dictionary.

Oxford Dictionary: The dictionary defines **Consciousness** - as the state of being; awareness, perception.

It defines 'mind' as

Oxford Dictionary: Mind - The seat of consciousness, thought, volition, and feeling. Attention, concentration. Intellectual powers.

Wow! Did you grasp those words in the same way I did? I interpret this as all those who have ADD or ADHD dis-orders already have their attention and concentration focused in the right direction. Now we all have a mind, so all we need to do is label ourselves with ADD or ADHD and we will begin tuning in, in the right direction. Although 'tuning in' would be the key here before you can dial.

Let us see what the dictionary says about this.

Oxford Dictionary: Tuning - The process or system of putting a musical instrument in tune.

Oxford Dictionary: Tune - A melody with or without harmony.

So then, I interpret this as 'we are the melody gaining harmony when we dial into this higher dimension'.

So dialling is making a connection, understanding this through the invention of the telephone. Before the telephone can dial you need to have a dial tone.

Oxford Dictionary: Tone – 1. Musical or vocal sound with reference to its pitch, quality and strength. 4. Be in harmony.

So a tone is a sound.

Oxford Dictionary: Sound - sound produced by continuous and regular vibrations.

So a certain harmonious vibrational frequency will give you access to transmit and receive. I know this as I have proved to myself that by changing my vibrational frequency from a negative one to a positive one I make the connection to a higher dimension. The only way I can explain that happening is by continuing with the telephone analogy.

A telephone is

Oxford Dictionary: Telephone – 1. An apparatus for transmitting sound. 2. Transmitting and receiving instrument used in 3. A system of communication using a network of telephones.

Well, we humans are physical instruments, so we are already a 'telephone', but having the telephone and not using it to dial out doesn't do much for us to gain access to messages.

Before we can dial we also need the correct number to dial. If dialling to the higher dimension is a spiritual connection, then I have the knowing within me that three and seven are spiritual numbers. But how do you input these numbers into us as telephones? By repeating positive vibrational actions, thoughts, or words, three or seven times. Continue repeating this and you will telepathically connect to the higher dimensions, going higher each time you redial.

I just had to consult the dictionary again on the word telepathy.

Oxford Dictionary: Telepathy - the supposed communication of thoughts or ideas otherwise than by the known senses.

Let us assume that the dictionary is right. I believe telepathy is the medium we will all use. We will rise beyond telephones and cell phones and it will be our known-or-unknown-senses that will lead us.

Goodness me, have any of you had so much fun with a dictionary and an open mind so early in the morning?

If you have also found the language and words of the Bible too difficult to understand, then perhaps all you need to BE is ADHD (Attention Dialled into a Higher Dimension) and read the Bible again (or the dictionary) just for the fun of it. I recommend you open your awareness first, before opening the Bible or a dictionary.

This then brings me to help you 'Be Aware' by explaining the purpose of hyphenating certain words like dis-ease, dis-order, dis-accordance. I first discovered this in Louise L. Hay's teachings. By creatively placing the hyphen in disease helps stimulate a new positive understanding. It triggers new thought patterns as you experience the energy of the words in a new-light, different from what you already know. It helps you to be aware that your disease now becomes a body that is not at ease. So it creates an ease, freedom and relief as you begin to feel the energy of the new hyphenated word. Your dis-ease is no longer so unhealthy and difficult to deal with.

Disorder then shifts to a new vibration when you create a new hyphenated word, dis-order. You begin to get the feeling that there is perfectly aligned order instead of your normal understanding of disorder.

Dis-accordance. I know this does not exist in any dictionary. I have created this word just for fun. I remember my English teacher at school told me I needed to create my own dictionary to go with all the new words I added into my stories. So, in accordance with all the rules we automatically conform to, perhaps there are times in life for dis-accordance.

I encourage you to go ahead and 'Ease, Order, Accordingly, in any life situation, without being **dis**tant from your own mind'.

But now I ask myself, as my mind wanders back to my past dis-eases, was there indeed a parasite that caused the bilharzia? Or was it, more accurately, a negative mental energy parasite?

Did my mind amazingly create a parasite that was picked up in a blood test? My wildly active mind now believes we all, with our own minds, create those germs that science can detect within our bodies and the environment.

Take a look at the flu virus. According to Louise L. Hay's teachings, this is a response to negativity and believing the statistics related to catching the flu.

Wow, do you understand this in the same way I do? If we all remove the negative thoughts we project, there will be no illnesses, or flu at least. The moment one person catches the flu, someone else does too. Why? Because we *talk* ourselves into *believing* we will also get sick. So negative, isn't it? The germ is a powerful negative thought pattern. Of course, this is also energy, carrying a vibration into a dense form, such as our bodies.

Oh, goodness me, I really must look up 'germ' in the dictionary:

131

Oxford Dictionary: Germ – 1. A micro-organism, esp. one which causes disease. 3. An original idea etc. from which something may develop; an elementary principle.

So there you have it, from the dictionary: Germ-an original idea-words that have existed in the dictionary for so long, waiting for us to dial into a higher dimension to interpret their vibrational message for our own highest good.

Self-Interpretation Of Metaphysical Fun

I am just truly having a whole lot of fun with an open mind in a higher dimension. Allow yourself to stretch your thought patterns and open your mind a little more; you never know what could come of it.   See how many new words you can create that will have a positive impact on your understanding of life.

Chapter 23 - Choices

(Age 36, year 2004)

New Year brings 2004 into existence. During a self-healing session, I know that I have another silent cyst lurking on my right ovary.

Being aware that I have only just released my deeply withheld secret of sexual abuse, I feel it needs to be checked out.

My doctor confirms an ovarian cyst. Thanks to the sonar screen, we can see it has an appearance which, when compared to the previous one, is abnormal. This time I agree to see the gynaecologist to have it tested. A quick in-and-out hospital visit is booked. The laparoscope and needle aspiration test will tell us the cell content.

I first take the time to meditate and do a self-healing in preparation for the day and acceptance of the chemical contamination from the anaesthetic. I have kept my body cleansed of all medications for a very long time and know that just one mild headache tablet knocks me out, with the effect of a strong sleeping tablet.

I ask Archangel Raphael, the healing archangel I often communicate with, to "Please assist both my doctor and gynaecologist through this procedure. Help to reduce the toxic effect within my physical body from the medication. Help me in dealing with the pain from cutting into my skin and muscles and, if possible, no pain at all."

I am well aware of the deep level of consciousness I have trained myself into achieving through meditation and healing. I am worried the anaesthetic and possibly medications may take me into a deeper state from which I may not have the ability to bring myself back. I take steps ahead of time to ensure I prevent this happening. I repeat to myself the positive thought pattern to prevent coma I have learned from Louise L. Hay's book.

It's Monday and I arrive at the hospital and undergo all necessary procedures and preparations. The cold theatre leaves me in shivers as my doctor sends me to sleep.

I awake in the ward, coughing and choking with a deep longing for my husband to be with me. He is not. I am alone in the ward. There is no pain at the point of operation. My throat is all that is sore, from coughing uncontrollably.

I can feel the pulling in my stomach with every cough. I know I need to stop coughing, before I pop open the stitches. I place my hands on my throat and begin healing, repeating the only words that pop into my mind, "I am loved and appreciated". About three minutes later my coughing begins to subside.

I am so thrilled that the anaesthetic has not caused a blockage within me to prevent the healing energies from flowing. I can still carry out healing on myself. This is amazing, and I am thankful. I give thanks to Archangel Raphael for helping me through this and, more important, for the absence of pain at the site of the operation.

Ready to go home, my husband and Casey arrive. The nurse informs me that pain medication has been prescribed to take home. I respond that I have very little pain so will not need it, and leave without the medication. I carefully walk out, along-side Casey and sense my husband's distance as he walks on ahead.

At home I go immediately to my healing bed to continue healing my throat which is sore and hoarse from all the coughing. Casey and Dustin sit next to me and share their first day back at school. Casey is excited about her new high school.

Deep inside, I am longing for some comfort and closeness from my husband as he sits in the lounge, and then prepares dinner for us. My emotions begin rising more strongly.

I discover a large amount of blood covering the plaster over my belly button. Just then, my doctor calls to find out how I am. My voice doesn't even sound like my own as we talk. He advises me to change the blood-drenched dressing and to apply pressure to stop the bleeding. I swallow hard, trying to avoid the tears settling in my eyes, the deep emotional energy catching in my throat.

I take a warm, relaxing bath and settle to apply a clean dressing to the wound. I am so pleased to have Casey helping me. I take my time applying pressure to the wound, until there is no more blood visible. As I relax in bed I watch my abdomen rising with discomfort and pressure. "I am just bloated," I tell myself. I know from previous anaesthetics that this can happen.

Then the pain begins increasing, fast and furious, and with rising nausea. My husband brings me a bucket, in-case I vomit. I ask him to please bring a tablet for the increasing pain. Sensing his boiling frustration towards me for not accepting the prescribed medication, I acknowledge I am just as annoyed with myself for refusing the stronger painkillers.

Later I rise from the bed to go to the toilet. I feel dizzy, the world floats all around me, sounds swirl in my head and I pass out.

I wake up on the end of my bed and slowly move into the middle, wondering what happened. Feeling weak, I know I have to go to the toilet, as pains strike through my entire abdomen. I lift myself more gently and slowly this time. I am out again. I wake up on the end of my bed once more.

Nausea turns to violent vomiting, pulling hard in my stomach and jolting my stitches. I am now very thankful for the bucket close by. The thoughts filter through my mind that I have been chemically poisoned, by the combination of anaesthetic and aspirin in the tablet I took, all too strong for my well-detoxed body to accommodate.

Feeling even weaker, I still have an urgency to go to the toilet. Taking it slower, thinking that perhaps I am just moving too fast, I feel the world spinning faster as I rise and I again collapse on the bed.

Too weak now to call my husband from the lounge, I decide to use my mental telepathy skills to call him to my aid. He appears immediately beside the bed, wondering what is wrong with me.

I weakly explain I keep passing out and need to go to the toilet, "Please help me," I ask.

He slowly helps me into a sitting position, where I again pass out. Regaining consciousness, I advise him he needs to get me to the hospital quickly as something has gone terribly wrong. Each time I lift my head I pass out, and I have gone from experiencing no pain to intense pain and pressure.

It is now around midnight and he insists on calling my doctor first. Fortunately my doctor instructs him to do so. We race off to the hospital, every bump and turn excruciating as I lie on the back seat of the car. My husband carries me into the emergency room.

The paramedic and doctor on duty attend to me. They set up a drip and prepare to admit me to a ward for further investigation. I explain to him my reaction to medications and the tablet I took earlier. I feel angry and fearful when they insist on transferring me to the ward in a wheelchair. I have already explained that I am unable to raise my head without passing out and that I can't sit up. Annoyed that they choose to ignore me, I am placed in the wheelchair only to pass out just as quickly.

I slowly regain consciousness and note they are wheeling me, in bed, to the ward. My husband leaves me in their care and returns home. The nurse explains that the doctor has instructed that x-rays be taken of my chest and abdomen.

I am resting while I wait for the radiology department to be opened. A little while later the nurse wheels me down to radiology and leaves me in the care of two other nurses. Time now for the x-rays, and the nurse explains I need to stand against the machine.

"Stand?" I ask. Listening to her confirming reply, I explain that when I raise my head, I pass out. She pulls a bench forward for me so I can sit against the machine.

"I can't lift my head," I repeat. After much persuading, the two nurses encourage me to attempt to sit as it will be over very quickly. I fearfully agree to attempt this with their close aid. I manage to sit and rise off the bed. As I begin to lift off the bed and turn to take a seat on the bench I feel my head swirling and a nurse's encouraging voice vanishing too quickly. "This is it, here I go, goodbye," I announce weakly to the nurses.

I am suddenly aware of something quite different from all the other times I passed out. I am aware I have passed out and I can actually see my limp body being held by both nurses.

I realise I am above them, above the whole scene, as if I am looking into a movie of my life. Strangely enough, I notice all my fears have vanished. I feel an increase in loving energy all around me and know the angels are here. I have a determined need to say goodbye to family and friends, knowing it is time for me to pass over. I appear over my children's beds at home, gently stroking their cheeks, saying goodbye. I squeeze my husband's hand; I fleetingly visit family all around the world saying a quick goodbye to each. I return to all my friends, watching them peacefully asleep, giving a gentle thought of goodbye. I visit my Reiki Masters who taught and attuned me into Reiki healing and share my love and appreciation with them, having the knowing within that they may be aware of my goodbye before anyone else. Escorted by a large team of guardian angels and archangels, I turn to Archangel Raphael and request my departure now.

I enter into a bright, tunnelled beam of light with all the colourful rays from the angels and archangels, I feel myself becoming lighter, cleansed and healed of all pain. I enter into conversation with Archangel Raphael.

"Tina, it is not your time to depart your physical body yet, but the choice is still yours," explains Archangel Raphael. "Well, why is this happening, if it is not my time?" I ask. "You are a healer and author, Tina, and it is your time to experience healing on all different levels, including this experience. It is time for others to do for you, too."

Archangel Raphael now stands beside Archangel Gabriel. "Tina, you still have much work to complete in this lifetime and you only need to decide if you want to return to continue it or not. You know your book is not complete and I would encourage you not to give up now. This experience will carry you through the next phase of your life, and your book. The choice is still yours," announces Archangel Gabriel.

"If I decide to return will I remember all this or not?" I ask. Archangel Raphael explains, "You will remember some of it, and we will ensure you remember all of it only when the time is right.

"Understand that your physical body is about to undergo further chemical contamination, lowering your energies, and I am here to help you at all times. You just need to ask."

"Okay, I will return, but can you heal my physical body as there is internal bleeding within it?"

"I am unable to heal it for you as I will be going against your Soul contract, as you are a healer and have chosen to help yourself, and to allow others to do for you through this experience. However, I can assist you and the others. Just remember and understand that your bleeding is internal. Upon entering your body, you will go into a weak, low state of energy for a very important and unique experience that you have chosen as a healer and you will not be aware of our presence, but we are definitely with you. You know what is happening inside your body; however, it is not for you to mention as you have to allow the doctors and all others to do what is necessary for you. This is also part of their purposes and experiences. Always remember, nothing will take place out of alignment with your Soul contract and you are definitely on track with your Soul purpose," encourages Archangel Raphael.

Archangel Gabriel adds, "I will be there to prompt you often with inspiration to keep on experiencing and sharing your healing example with many others through your book". We continue on in deep personal conversation.

Feeling a strong vibration of love and knowingness, which I absorbed through this experience, I turn and know exactly where I need and choose to be. I immediately feel myself descending and entering my body.

Becoming conscious, I hear one nurse shout to another, "Call the doctor, quickly," as they lift me onto the bed. Placing me on my side I feel my body shaking and jerking, with uncontrollable vomiting and diarrhoea at the same time. Within moments the doctor on duty is sternly telling me to breathe deeply. I am feeling too weak to breathe and I feel something in my mouth. Trying hard to focus on breathing, I notice how limp and weak my body is. I remember from my Louise L. Hay book that bleeding is "joy running out". I silently repeat to myself, "I accept joy and circulate it through every part of my body." Aware now of what Archangel Raphael meant by, "Just remember and understand, your bleeding is internal," that it is not running out, but is running within."

The doctor asks, "Have you ever had an epileptic fit or convulsion like this before?" "No," I reply weakly. I hear the doctor instruct I be taken back to the ward and have some blood tests before x-rays are attempted again. I'm still on my side, with my eyes closed, thinking I need to remember all this for my book, as my bed is pushed back to the ward. The nurse attends to cleaning me and changing all sheets.

I feel such an intense gratitude towards this nurse and her dedication to her duties. I drift in and out of sleep, aware of the nurse checking on me often.

At dawn on Tuesday a short lady stands beside me and introduces herself as my new surgeon, explaining that my doctor has requested she take over my care. She instructs that a sonar be done.

This time the radiologist makes a plan to x-ray me flat on the bed, finally acknowledging that I am unable to lift my head. With this task successfully completed quite quickly, I am pushed into the sonar room.
The radiologist places the cold gel on my abdomen and begins. Her eyes widening as she gasps at what she sees.

"We have finally found the problem, now we can help you. Let me call the doctor quickly," she says. She leaves the room and returns with the doctor immediately. The doctor introduces himself, and begins his job in haste. He explains, "Your entire abdomen is filled with fluid. Look," he shows me, "All your organs are floating." I glance sideways at the screen, fascinated to see my organs moving as he presses on my fluid-filled abdomen.

139

Back in the ward, the surgeon arrives. She explains that I will need to go into theatre urgently to have the fluid removed. She explains that this could be blood from the wounds from yesterday's tests on the ovary.

While waiting in the ward for my approaching op, I think back to the events of my out-of-body experience.

What had probably been a couple of minutes during which I had passed out in our time zone felt more like hours that I was within the astral plane, saying goodbye and floating and chatting with the archangels, truly experiencing a different reality altogether.

Eventually, in my very weak state, I drift off to a deep sleep, unaware of being taken into theatre.

I awake in the intensive care unit, equipment attached to me and a nurse wiping down my body. I hear beeping sounds all around me. I slowly open my eyes and glance around, absorbing my surroundings. Intensive care, I announce to myself, taking time to truly connect my thoughts, awareness and words to where I am.

"How are you?" the nurse greets my open eyes with compassion. Weakly, I look at her and close my eyes again, too weak to talk, or think about how I am. Later, more awake, I become aware of a headache. She wipes my face with a warm cloth and brings my attention back to her as my eyes open again. I relax, allowing my body to be taken care of by others. I am becoming more aware of the pain throbbing in my head and abdomen. Drips, drains, catheter, spare medication pipes, machines, clamp on my finger and an oxygen mask are all attached to my body.

My attending surgeon visits. "How are you, Tina?" I weakly reply, "My head is sore." She explains that pain medication will start now and leaves for the night.

I ask the nurse for water. "No, sorry, you are not allowed to take anything through the mouth," she replies. "Can I have some ice?" I ask. "No, you can't." Her reply weakens me further. I allow my mind and body to rest.

140

By Wednesday morning I am completely awake. My surgeon explains what had actually happened.

"You had a very large amount of internal bleeding in your abdomen, which pushed up and squashed your lungs. The bleeding was from all your internal wounds. We had to temporarily remove your colon to drain the blood, clean you, and re-stitch the bleeding wounds. We need to give you transfusions as you have lost an incredible amount of blood. You are not allowed to take anything by mouth as your colon needs to remain dormant for some time to prevent paralysis, which is normal after moving the colon. This big white bag of liquid is your food; you're being fed through one of the many pipes attached to your shoulder. We will be starting physio this morning so that you can build strength and deepen your breathing, using all of your lung capacity. Your breathing is still very weak and you need to keep your oxygen mask on all the time. We are giving you medication for the pain. I waited to speak to your husband last night after your surgery but he was not here, please can you tell him on my behalf."

I now understand why breathing is so difficult. More regularly now the nurse wakes me, reminding me to breathe as I seem to keep forgetting. The machine is beeping wildly, as a warning. What an effort it is to breathe, something we all take for granted.

I glance down and take a look at my body for the first time. Shock radiates through me as I see how swollen and white I am, my arms and hands look nothing like my own. I appear to have gained an instant 15 kgs.

My doctor visits. "How are you, Tina?" I just look at him, weakly, over the top of my oxygen mask. "I was here with you after your surgery last night, waiting for you to wake up and you didn't, so I eventually left. I was looking for my husband in the waiting room but he was not here, so we have not been able to tell him what happened to you." He gives me a compassionate concerned look, pats my arm, says "goodbye" and departs, leaving me to rest.

Later my husband visits and I explain what had happened. I ask him to bring a pen and my journal the next time he visits, to contact my friends and to ask some trinity healers to please come by to do a healing on me. I am uncomfortable about the blame and anger he has towards the gynaecologist for all that has happened to me. I am so aware of energies and I would prefer to focus on positive, uplifting vibrations, not negative ones, at this stage. I am completely filled with gratitude for being alive and want to remain in this positive state. I know better than to blame anyone for the events that have occurred, as it was all part of my journey. I have a new and very deep understanding of this since my out-of-my body experience. I don't want to lose this deep love inside, by becoming attached to negative energy.

My first blood transfusion begins. I am silent and grateful to accept this blood. "Your temperature is very high," the nurse explains with a concerned glance. She is wiping down my body with a cool face-cloth and has a fan blowing on me. There is no success in lowering my temperature.

My surgeon visits and, with great concern, instructs the nurses not to continue with the second batch of blood until my temperature has normalised.

I automatically attempt to carry out Reiki. I weakly lift my hands and place them on my abdomen, ready to let healing energy circulate in and around my body. I am well aware there is no energy coming out of my hands. Tears arise with a flood of emotions as I know I am truly not meant to be doing this for myself this time round. I feel so weak and defeated.

A little later I sense the presence of my two Reiki Masters beside me, doing distant healing. I am so pleased that my sense of awareness is still strongly active and I know they are with me. I allow them to do this healing for me. I am thankful that in their awareness and following their intuition, they know I am in need of extra help.

The nurse later confirms to me that my temperature has lowered and the fan is switched off. My doctor visits and I am now able to greet him with a smile, much stronger than during his previous visit. I ask him if some trinity healers will be allowed into intensive care to do some healing for me. "No problem and it's good to see you have your smile back on your face again," he says.

My husband visits and mentions that my Reiki Masters phoned and asked what had happened to me, and that they have already done distant healing. I am thankful for this confirming news. He places my pen and journal, to record these events for my book, on my bedside table, along with my 'Heal Your Body' by Louise L. Hay. He also lets me know that my friends and trinity healers will come by later.

The physio therapist arrives with my nurse and announces: "You have to sit up now, as we need to teach you how to breathe again," she laughs. I refuse to sit, "No, I don't want to," I announce. The nurse reaches her hand out to me and explains. "You are just fearful of sitting because of all the times you passed out." I know she is right. She reassures me, "You will not pass out this time, you have progressed a lot since then and your blood pressure is stable enough for you to sit." She leaves me for a while to deal with my fears. When she returns she smiles at me. "I think we will allow you to remain in bed for this first time. We will just lift you a little." They do so, and I discover that I am able to lift my head and remain conscious. What a relief! The physio begins with focusing on breathing just a little deeper.

I am left to rest and I watch the nurses carrying out their duties in silence.

My trinity healers come to do a healing on me and I smile weakly and gratefully. The nurse explains to them that if the machine begins beeping it is indicating that the percentage level of oxygen has dropped and they must remind, me urgently, to breathe again. They stand around my bed beaming energy towards me and I relax and absorb it all.

As they depart the nurse checks my temperature and I can feel the change in my body. "Goodness," she says, "it has lowered." We smile at each other, knowing this is a result of the healing.

Curious, she asks me all about my friends and their healing, and my healing books on the bedside counter. I tell her about the power of natural healing. I discover I have no enthusiasm to read or attempt to write my own book. Recovery is all I have strength for.

The third day, Thursday, begins with a second blood transfusion. A new bag of white food replaces the empty one. My temperature again skyrockets as the new blood enters my body. I can feel the heat radiating from my body. I think of how grateful I am that someone took the time to donate the blood that is flowing into my body. That 'somebody' will not even be aware that what they did some time ago is helping me at this very moment.

The nurse checks my temperature and is concerned again. I complain about the severe headache I still have. Medication is not helping. Still not allowed anything to drink, I am given large lemon swab sticks to suck on to lubricate my very dry lips and mouth. I am grateful that I can at least have these, although they're not quite as satisfying as water, especially as I love to drink plenty of water every day. I have not drunk anything for three days. Although my body is absorbing fluid through the drip, my mouth totally disagrees with this torture.

The physio visits with a smile on her face, insisting I sit today on the chair. First I have to wear these splendid designer stockings without feet, to prevent blood clots. I notice how my pale skin blends with these white stockings. I know I have to conquer my fear this time and allow myself to sit in a chair. She assists me into a sitting position on the comfortable armchair. I am given a breathing apparatus as a 'toy' to practice deepening each breath. My initial target is 250 ml. With much effort, I soon achieve this. Physio continues, relieving some pressure still lurking around my abdomen as I re-learn how to focus on controlled breathing.

I reflect on my life, and on how I managed to take all the deep breathing techniques I learnt in meditation for granted. I realise, too, how we all take our breathing for granted. At this stage breathing is still very difficult for me. With toy in hand and physio finished, I practice breathing on my own with complete focus every half hour. I have accepted spending the day sitting up in the chair. The nurse has explained how important this is for recovery, providing the lungs with space to breathe.

I have progressed to using the oxygen mask only when I sleep.

I drift off to sleep in the chair, oxygen mask tied to my face, being woken up every now and again by the nurse and the beeping oxygen machine whenever my breathing becomes too shallow. I force myself to find the strength to use my breathing toy to increase the oxygen in my blood, and then go back to sleep.

With perfect timing my trinity healers appear again, six of them today. They are pleased to see me sitting. They proceed in healing and I just enjoy it, absorbing all the energy I can, ensuring I don't forget to breathe deeper and deeper. They all depart and have once again accomplished an important task, lowering my temperature during the transfusion. The healing has given me an incredible amount of strength. I spend the rest of the day in the chair, awake.

My husband and Jane visit and are impressed with my progress, even the colour sweeping back into my skin as I absorb more blood. My husband is expressing his anger at the gynaecologist. I find myself wishing he would go home for now, as I am still too weak to experience negative energies at this time. I don't think he realises how sensitive and aware I really am. I long to just be left alone, so I can focus on gaining strength with all the love still residing deep within me.

Late afternoon, my body feeling very tired and weak from sitting all day, I ask the nurse to lift me back into bed so I can sleep a little more comfortably. She helps me onto the bed and I relax back and sleep for a while. With a very stable temperature, my third and final blood transfusion begins and continues through the night.

Friday morning I am much stronger and sitting more comfortably in the armchair. I focus my attention on the nurses carrying out their duties in silence and dedication to their patients, and the large amount of recording there is, for every procedure must be documented on the charts.

My attention is caught as I feel panic rushing through the nurse opposite me and alarms sound loudly through the intensive care unit. All nearby nurses are suddenly rushing around; my own nurse runs across the room; those at the central nurse-station, the head nurse, all dropping currently important activities and rushing to the bedside of a man in critical condition.

I immediately know this man is having a heart attack. A doctor runs in and takes over. Everybody is attuned to this emergency; the doctor pumps his chest. Oxygen is pumped into his mouth by a nurse. The heart-shocking machine (defibrillator) is applied and fired as everybody stands back. I can feel the tension in the air. I raise my hands to attempt beaming healing energy across the room toward the doctor. The doctor happens to look and connect with me for a second or two. I realise there is no energy leaving my hands again. I should not be doing this now and instead pray for all of them. I have the inner knowing that it is the doctor and nurses who are in need of assistance. The man has already taken departure, under the care of his own spiritual guides and guardian angels.

I remember I was at that same place some days ago and I just know he has gone all the way. Knowing it is his time to go and that no-body can change that. It was his choice. My gaze is locked with that of the doctor, whose shirt is wet with sweat as he continues trying to save his patient.

I notice how aware my senses are, and how accurate, from this distance. For the first time I am up close and personal with a dedicated doctor coping with a hopeless emergency. He is not at all willing to give up, even as a nurse places her hand on his shoulder and shakes her head as if she, too, knows this man is beyond help.

Finally, the doctor stands back in exhaustion and defeat. He shakes his head, emotions sweep through him. He switches off all machines and lights; everybody departs and closes the curtains; the body is left in the dark.

I talk to my nurse as she returns to me, "Did that man just die of a heart attack?" I ask. She nods yes, but quickly announces "I am not allowed to discuss that with you." I had caught her off-guard but received the confirmation I needed. I notice her emotions and distress. She continues, in silence, trying desperately to focus on her paperwork at the end of my bed.

I realise how so many of us take for granted what goes on in others and all around us. Here in intensive care everybody, especially the nurses, is expected to just swallow the natural human emotion and continue in well-practiced routine, as if nothing has happened. I am very sensitive to the complete energy change in the entire intensive care unit. Everybody has felt what has happened. Every single nurse has been moved by this death, no matter how often they may have encountered such events.

A short while later the man's wife is escorted in with a relative. She goes behind the curtains alone to say her farewell and leaves emotionally weak, barely able to walk.

Soon all the nurses, in a precise sweeping motion, close the curtains around all the beds in intensive care, while the body is removed. I continue talking to the archangels, to help everyone present at this event and in this ward to deal with the emotion appropriately.

I am so impressed with their dedication to duty, working through their own exhaustion to perfection. I wonder how many people are truly grateful for what these nurses do.

My breathing is improving incredibly but, using my oxygen mask at night only, my breathing target has shifted to 750 ml and I am only able to reach 500 ml. Back in bed for the night, I have the very best deep sleep for the first time in intensive care.

My fifth morning, Saturday, is welcomed with the news of my transfer into a ward. I am first given a small glass of apple juice to drink. Taking a very small, slow sip for the first time in five days is awesome. I enjoy the cold, wet feeling and sweet taste on my lips. I hold the juice in my mouth for a while before swallowing. This is the height of gratitude: I'm finally allowed to drink.

In the ward I am so grateful to see the sun dazzling through the windows again, a very different atmosphere from that in intensive care. I expect to start eating soon and to go home on Monday. My daily physio and practice with my breathing toy is helping me tremendously. In the ward I progress fast. The catheter is removed and I am helped to stand and begin walking again. It takes some time to master walking with two drip stands and a bag of blood still draining from my abdomen. I am grateful for having the drip stands to hold onto through some of my weak moments. The dressing over my stitches is removed to reveal a raw, open wound of infection, an allergic reaction to the plaster, apparently due to the low white blood cell count from loss of blood. My wound is left open to heal. I am given the good news that I can begin eating soft, liquid foods. Of greater excitement is that my children are now allowed to visit me. I wait anxiously for visiting hours to come around. In they walk with my husband, happiness flooding through me as they give me a big hug. Each excitedly tells me all about school and their new teachers. I still feel my husband's anger, as he is just unable to accept and let go of what the gynaecologist had done. I try hard not to allow his anger to get to me. Visiting hours over and everyone gone, I am very weak and tired, battling to find any strength. I am struggling with the thoughts and resistance I have towards my husband's continued anger each time he visits. I am ready to sleep but the nurse checking on me notices my difficulty in breathing again and insists I sleep with the oxygen mask on for the night.

After a long, tiring night up and down to the toilet, Sunday arrives. I am exhausted and in need of plenty more sleep. My tiredness is temporarily pushed aside as I welcome my first meal in six days. Sloppy porridge and juice is all I am allowed, but I am grateful to be eating again. After three spoons, I am full. The nurse inspects how much porridge I have eaten and notices that the porridge was the wrong texture, not as sloppy as it should have been. Her concern strikes an inner realisation and panic rises. She watches me as I feel intense discomfort in my abdomen, which develops into excruciating pains. The physio is called to assist with the intense pain. A vibrating machine is left strapped to me to relax my muscles. My surgeon rushes in and confirms a 'paralysis of the colon' from eating food a little too textured for my colon to handle.

I remain resting until just before evening visiting hours. I again go to the toilet with the help of the nurses. Pain and tears weaken me more as I struggle to walk back to the ward. Just then my husband, Casey, Dustin and my parents arrive. Everyone is so shocked to see I have been knocked back into a weakened and painful state. The nurses help me back into bed.

Feeling very weak, I struggle to focus on those visiting and soon extreme nausea rises fast and strongly turns into uncontrollable vomiting. I weakly rest my head back, embarrassed that this all has happened during visiting hours and everyone in the ward has seen it. I am relieved and tired when visiting hours are over. The pain medication now makes me drowsier than it is actually relieving pain. I fall asleep for most of the night, once again not allowed to eat or drink anything.

Monday morning and I'm feeling much better, without pain. The surgeon orders repeat sonar and x-rays to check my colon. I am disappointed to hear my stay in hospital has been prolonged.

Medication is prescribed to activate my colon again. My doctor visits and gives me the results of the tests the gynaecologist did on my ovarian cyst. The good news is it is only a cyst, which I need to do healing on.

By day-break on Tuesday, my colon has still not become active, so I have to stay in hospital for another two days. The good news is the drain in my abdomen is removed one less item to carry around. What a pleasure it is now to walk! I begin exercising more, walking around the ward helps my colon to become active. I am slowly introduced back onto fluids again. My breathing has increased to 1000 ml now, a remarkable improvement, although the target for my age is 2500 ml. My day turns out to be most enjoyable. I am able to meditate quite well again and keep my thoughts positive. I keep myself filled with gratitude and love. I am in high spirits. I take the time to read, write and continue my breathing exercises. I no longer need the oxygen mask. By late afternoon my colon becomes active. The best news is I am now allowed to begin eating again. I am given soup and very sloppy ice-cream. My body digests this well. Pain medication is reduced. I have a wonderful night's sleep.

Wednesday, my ninth day, is welcomed with the news that I will be allowed to go home at the end of the day. The drip is finished and the nurse comes to remove all tubes. "This may be a little uncomfortable," she announces. I look down at my shoulder while she cuts open the two stitches holding the tubes in place. She begins pulling, I feel major discomfort deep in the middle of my chest and I place my hand over it. "This tube has been feeding the food directly into your heart," she confirms. I watch her pulling and pulling; I am shocked to see how long it is. Finally it is out and I am left with a lot of discomfort. My husband, Casey and Dustin arrive to take me home. It feels so good to be home, I settle down to relax, knowing my healing journey continues.

Learning how to eat solids again proves to be very painful, as my colon adjusts and gains strength. My healing energies are slowly strengthening as my body detoxes from all medications. It takes three months for me to regain my full strength of healing energy and my body to be completely detoxified of all the morphine I was given.

Self-Interpretation Of Choices

We all get to choose how to experience our life events. I could also choose to blame the gynaecologist. However, I chose to be grateful that I am still alive and have experienced all that I have.

Probably the combination of longing for my husband to be with me and the physical insertion of tubes into my lungs during the op added to all the coughing. Clearly the amount of coughing I did certainly jolted all the internal stitches and caused all the bleeding.

I had begun containing and suppressing my anger towards my husband for not being present when I came out of theatre. This continued at home, with my anger increasing as I noticed my husband ignoring me. But deep inside me there was a huge store of joy.

I pushed aside this anger and tried to focus on resting, not wanting to accept his distance from me when I was longing for his comforting hug.

Notice how my doctor happened to call just when I was determined to push aside dealing with the distance from my husband; certainly pushing out my tears. The dizziness soon began.

I was doing all I could not to look at the truth of my relationship with my husband and the growing distance between us. Of course, the loss of blood added to this dizziness.

Fear was building; I was aware that something did not feel right. I begin feeling guilty for thinking he was ignoring me when he 'caringly' brought me a bucket, and a tablet that could well have added to the increasing pain.

I began hating myself again for refusing the stronger pain medication prescribed. Although I believed my refusal could have been a big blessing, as the stronger medication may have just been too strong, and I could have passed out and into a deeper state of unconsciousness, or even the coma of which I was so fearful.

The violent vomiting was embodied a rejection of what was happening to me. I also believe my body was beginning a natural detox for what was ahead: another anaesthetic and further chemical contamination.

I clearly was rejecting life in that moment, through my request to pass over during my out-of-body experience. The vomiting and diarrhoea was caused by fear and rejection. The breathing problems were not only caused by pressure on the lungs from internal bleeding but, more importantly, brought me back to focus on my husband, who I believed did not want to be around me. My feeling was that he no longer loved me. I managed to focus on the gratitude I had gained, and again avoided my feelings.

My surgeon just had to bring to my attention that my husband was not at the hospital waiting to hear how my surgery had gone. I pushed aside any thought of my husband not being there for me once again, probably in denial of the truth because I did not want to face it.

My doctor ensured that he, too, brought up the fact of my husband not being around during my operation. I did my best to make excuses for him, but deep down I felt so rejected and unloved. I was being guided to love myself more.

My husband's visit hit the tip of the iceberg within me when I had to face his concern, which was focused on blaming the doctor about what had happened, rather than on how I was. I noticed a pattern of attraction there, a repeat of when I crashed his company car and after the attempted hijacking.

My transformation from a dependent relationship was now shifting greatly. I managed to force myself to focus on gratitude, and I understood why he was angry at the doctor, which was replaying some of his trauma in childhood and reflected his anger. So I was able to understand and forgive him.

The headache that continued and was not cleared by the medication was unexplainable by the surgeon. This was, I believe, a reflection of my own self-criticism.

An important point I want to make for anyone visiting another in hospital or when ill is the impact of the energies you bring with you. Without a doubt, whether the person is sensitive and aware or not, they will be affected by your energies and attitude.

Chapter 24 – Friend Soulmates

(Age 36, year 2004)

Once upon a time in a bright starry sky there were two wise Souls preparing for and planning their next life-time.

"How will I know to find you?" asks one small, powerful, bright Soul to the other. "We do have such an amazingly powerful task in this lifetime and we truly do need to meet each other. We will need to motivate and encourage each other, and share our experiences."

"I know," says the other. "Each of us needs to take half of the love in our hearts, half of the lessons we have already learnt, half of our Soul, half of our bright lights within, and give it to each other now, before we begin this next life. Then when we are truly ready to meet, after having gained and learnt our own new lessons and wisdom, all we need to do is go into our own hearts and Souls and reflect our bright light out into the universe. Then the other will beam their heart and Soul's brightness and, together, the powerful, mirrored beam of light shall attract and unite us. When we align the beam directly through our hearts and Souls we will just know that we have found the other half of ourselves. From that moment on, we will feel even more complete and whole. We will truly shine our power out into the world for the highest good of all other Souls. Far greater will be our need to continue to feed it, with love and care. We will be feeding each other's Souls."

One last thought: "Perhaps we also need to choose similar names?"

"Good idea. I will choose Tiela and begin my journey first, okay?"

"I will choose Tina and stay here a little longer to watch over you."

"I'm ready," says Tiela, giving and sharing her half, and accepting my half.

And so it begins......

Self-Interpretation Of Friend Soulmates

This is just an inner-child story reflecting the choices before birth to meet other people; friendly Soulmates in this case.

I encourage you to remember your plans to meet and share your experiences with those in your life.

Tiela and I are aware and amazed in the so-called 'co-incidental' way in which we met and experience life with many similarities.

It was truly amazing to meet Tiela for the first time, or perhaps I should say, in this life-time. The powerful way in which we talked and connected, as if we had known each other for a long time; to discover, instantly, how much we have in common; and to truly feel so comfortable together.

How wonderful it is to share our similar and sometimes simultaneous events with each other, to experience the fun, joy and laughter with such amazement.

Chapter 25 - Cross Roads

(Age 36, year 2004)

Imminent divorce from my husband emerges and I meet with fears of financial insecurity. I now need to take on financial responsibilities alone and I am aware I am not earning enough to go it alone.

"What am I to do now to financially survive in this world, God? Do I give-up my Reiki practice completely and walk back into the corporate world, just for money? It would be the sensible thing to do, for my security and that of my children. Do I truly give up all of this that I have created?"

I feel and hear the immediate answers directly within me.

"No need to jump into fears through a lack of money. Relax, take your time and enjoy the experience. All will be provided for you; money is not all that is necessary to survive. You know this already, you have experienced your difficulties and your own tests over the last three years with absolute success. You know that love replaces all, provides all. You have actually experienced financial success, just not in the way you expected. It has always arrived just as you need it. You only need an extra abundance of trust, faith and direction, which is now supplied. Maintain your level of calmness and serenity and don't make hasty decisions."

Days follow during which I attempt to find a job as a personal assistant. Nothing is available for me; it is the end of the year with very few suitable positions available.

I completely surrender to trust and faith that something will be sent directly to me.

I visit a friend for dinner and a really welcome break from the stress of this divorce journey. I sit on her couch, situated under two lights. While we talk one of the lights goes out. We both look at this light and kind of shrug it off, and continue talking and enjoying each other's company. I talk about my confusion in not knowing what I should be doing anymore. We also talk about a South African magazine; and suddenly the light comes back on. We both look at this in amazement.

"Wait a moment, what were we just talking about," I excitedly say to her. "The light has just come on to give me a sign, it is shining light on something for me to see." My words bubble out of me in haste. We go over our discussion and clarify. "The magazine, there is something for you in the magazine, a new path perhaps," her own psychic abilities are in full swing, delivering the message I need to hear. I still don't know what, though. I am only just beginning my venture into writing my book, so what could I possibly do at a magazine company? The evening passes with so much enjoyment and wonderful conversations.

A couple of nights later I have a confirming dream of direction. My conversation within the dream is crystal clear. *I'm talking to the lady who handles the advertising in the magazine and she tells me, "There is a position available here for you."*

I wake from this dream and I feel its intensity of direction and know that I must not ignore this. I contact the company.

I visit a nearby crystal shop. I walk in and am greeted by the sight of this particular magazine on display. I reach out and take a copy to purchase. I search through all the books for sale, knowing there are hidden messages waiting to leap out at me, just as this magazine stood before my eyes. I leave the shop with my magazine in hand.

At home I sit in anticipation to see what this magazine has within for me. The magazine slides off my lap and falls to the floor, open at an article: 'Get a life coach'. This, too, is a repetitive sign, on life coaching, that has been coming to me.

I follow through with this sign too, and phone to enquire and then book a space for my coaching.

I allow myself to trust all the signs.

That evening I receive an email from the co-owner of the magazine. They are currently looking for a personal assistant who is in touch with body, mind and spirit. I sit back in gratitude, as this is unbelievable. I feel a tug within my Soul as I question whether I really need to return to the position of personal assistant. I agree to just 'go with the flow' because I know that if I am truly meant to move forward in this direction, it will unfold exactly as it is meant to.

I attend my life coaching appointment. This proves to be a leap in further releasing my marriage and accepting divorce.

Direction is pointed out, loud and clear, through a simple, silent moment in nature, connected through a small piece of Christmas tree twig. I pull it off and interpret the message I am receiving.

"No matter what choices you make in your life, your Soul purpose is within you. You are always guided on your path. There is no wrong choice."

Returning in-doors and to the group circle, I choose a guidance card.

The card says: Opportunity – *Sometimes the solutions to our problems are right under our noses. What opportunities are you not seeing or choosing to see? Take meaningful action on an opportunity that presents itself today.*

Powerful clarification blooms and blossoms in my mind. I now understand my signs and feelings of moving forward into life coaching, and realise this is to unfold from and through this book.

Two weeks later I am invited to attend the interview for personal assistant. My instant feelings are yes; this is your direction, Tina. I avoid any questioning and completely trust this as divine guidance. Days later I am offered the position and I accept with so much gratitude.

Self-Interpretation Of Cross Roads

By surrendering to my fear I managed to unlock many blockages. I discovered all the answers are within us.

I attracted all events and signs leading the way here. I now know my intuition is in full development. How patient our guides truly are to continually assist in sending us signs leading the way, over and over, until we finally get it and become more aware.

Chapter 26 - Spiritual Growth

(Age 36, year 2004)

The morning of Christmas Eve is here with the sweet sound of the birds in the tree beside my bedroom window, my yellow curtain gently swaying in the warm breeze of fresh air flowing through.

I think how amazingly attuned to the universe the birds are, how detached from electrical equipment, as they begin singing at the same time every morning without any alarm clock. I relax in bed and reflect on the year of intense growth and change that has unfolded with increased speed.

My divorce proceedings are still in action and all the lessons that go with it pound in my heart for even more attention than I have given them. The greatest challenge is about to begin. For the first time in 18 years, Christmas and New Year will be without my husband. Casey and Dustin, asleep in their beds are unaware of my thoughts, my emotions and even fears of conquering half of Christmas Day totally alone when they spend time with their dad and his family.

My thoughts lead me deeper into the emotions I have been holding back. It is time for me to accept that sometimes with divorce in-laws choose to depart from you too. I am so accustomed to spending Christmas Day with them, sharing the love, joy, laughter and Christmas spirit. My family has changed; many parts of my life have changed.

My tears flow good and strong and I just allow myself to enjoy the moment of emotional cleansing, knowing how much I shall shift through this. I end the fall into an emotional pit and sit within my daily Merkaba meditation. Feeling brighter, happier and more peaceful, I have the strength to take on this day.

For the first time this season there is a small spark of enthusiasm for Christmas shifting up within me. I decide it is time to create a new tradition with my children in the way we celebrate Christmas. Our past years have been focused on giving gifts at Christmas, rather than the true spirit of love.

Recent stressful conflict from the divorce has eroded all of our spirits. But now I see the gift within the conflict; it provides a golden opportunity for healing relationships and a coming together. This gift of conflict happens to be perfectly timed.

Having not had the financial means to focus Christmas on many material purchases is just another wonderful gift.

I go ahead and plan the evening. This year Casey and Dustin will stay up late and welcome Christmas Day in at midnight. They feel the shift out of their comfort zone just a little too much. They still want to wake up in the morning to many presents under the tree, as in the past. I explain that there are very few presents this year, but there is one very special one we can create together and give to one another. I keep them in suspense for the evening, not telling them what I am preparing. They begin allowing themselves to accept this change in tradition as we settle down together and watch TV until 11:30. We switch off TV and I gather my angel cards, candles and incense. We sit on a blanket in the lounge, in a circle around the candles. I explain that Christmas should be more about the gift of love than material gifts, a time for family to come together, rather than part. Unfortunately our family as we have known it in the past has changed, we are separate. I sense Casey and Dustin feeling their disappointment as they begin to think that I have truly not been able to afford Christmas gifts for them this year as I focus more on the gift of love instead. I share my feelings with them as we continue talking and finally move forward into forgiving one another for all the conflicts we have created in our relationships with one another recently. Now past midnight, Christmas morning, I share with them a recent miracle that came my way. I explain the importance of prayer and show them prayers are answered. Just a couple of days ago I had no money to purchase food, so gifts for them were far from any reality.

But I made sure of asking for gifts to give them in my prayers. My prayers were immediately answered with conflict, which didn't appear to be much of a gift at the time. Then followed some money, just enough to purchase very small gifts for them. I chose some clothes.

Finally their eyes brighten up as I hand them their presents. They also receive money and clothes from granny and grandpa, who are also not with us this year. I feel satisfied in having first given them the greatest gift of all, love through communication and forgiveness, and just being together. Our excitement settles as we decide it is time to sleep, and we agree to sleep together in the lounge on a mattress, completely out of routine. For the first time in 18 years we sleep-in late on Christmas morning and, upon waking, we watch a Christmas movie, again so different from our past Christmases. The time comes for Casey and Dustin to leave with their dad to celebrate the rest of Christmas, with a wonderful lunch at their aunt and uncle's home. As they leave we exchange big, tender hugs. I feel my emotions tugging, and know my time alone has arrived.

I feel the huge separation, not just from the children, but more importantly from those who have been my family for the past 18 years, and who have chosen not to even contact me with a telephone call.

I realise how tough these lessons are. Fortunately I know these are powerful spiritual lessons which, used wisely, will shift me in leaps and bounds. Trying to avoid the tears and heartache, I keep myself busy with housework. The emotional pull is just too strong now. The moment I allow myself to surrender, I hit rock bottom, into such deep heartache, my tears creating a strong, flowing river down my cheeks.

So many thoughts just empty themselves automatically, a conscious thought or two of guidance and support filtering in to remind me that letting go of grief is necessary for growth and cleansing.

I realise now how important it was that the universe arrange this year's season for me to be totally alone. All my friends and family are away on holiday, allowing me time to myself. I shift emotionally, feeling the peace coming over me after such deep release.

Be Aware

My suppressed laughter is suddenly bubbling to the surface. I am amused at the strange arrangement I have of living in a suburb called Cinderella, and feeling just like Cinderella in a fairy-tale, doing housework on Christmas Day when everyone else is truly having a ball without me around. They are all enjoying a wonderful feast, with roast turkey, roast pork, roast potatoes, rice, cauliflower and mouth-watering cheese sauce, followed by Christmas pudding. My taste buds are tingling. I realise how pathetic I am being, by choosing to do housework on such a beautiful day as this. I make myself a sandwich, grateful that I have at least something to eat, and venture into the garden to enjoy the fresh air.

My sleeping bag opened out on the grass, I sit in the middle, alone. I enjoy my sandwich and realise how satisfied I am with it. I don't need to eat much food. I begin a repeat of my Merkaba meditation. I notice the shifts taking place on all levels, spiritually, emotionally, mentally, and physically. I grin to myself, truly knowing the meaning of spiritual growth and that it is not an easy task, and that we need to go through it to experience it all. Some-time later I open my eyes to welcome my three cats who have joined me on my sleeping bag. Smurfie is Dustin's grey cat, Snuggles is Casey's black and white cat, and Panda is my black cat. I cuddle each one, realising I do have family with me. I am not alone. Panda notices the movement in the grass as the sleeping bag cord moves, with Snuggles tugging the other end. Ears perked high and with full focused attention, Panda shifts his body and prepares for launch. With a wagging of his behind he leaps upon the end of the cord. Snuggles leaps in fright, her focus distracted by Panda's pounce. Panda flops down on his side with the cord grasped in all paws, kicking wildly with his rear paws in his playful attack. Smurfie, usually too grumpy to pay attention, slowly lifts his head to all the action. I smile, realising what a joyful and playful moment this is. I pull the cord from Panda, as well as the other one, which has gone unnoticed. Throwing it back and forth, Smurfie gracefully joins in. For the first time all three of them play together, without any wild claws and hissing fights. I wonder if this is perhaps not a sign for me that peace is here and all conflicts have been resolved. I also know that it is temporary, if I intend to grow and ascend my consciousness further. I spend a great deal of time playing and truly enjoying myself. Our playful fun ends with a loud blast of thunder up above as the clouds gather together, all three cats scattering in their own directions. The opening of the grey clouds showers me with large and fast raindrops. I jump up with sleeping bag in hand and run in-doors.

I stretch out on the couch to watch more Christmas movies, just to meet with more tears as the movies relate to my experience of broken families. I feel so down again and understand the importance of change; the importance of being grateful for all the happy and sad times, and to truly appreciate all my moments.

I think how much work goes on behind the scenes for all of us to experience life within divine timing. How important is the flow of my ups and downs, which have been carefully planned. The thunder and rain had to appear at that precise moment to take me from my up moment of being, to back down, in tears, through a movie. How many of us are aware and grateful for this behind the-scenes work. This is when you know that God is working in your life, answering your prayers and even ignoring some, to ensure you learn and grow just as you need to.

Finally Casey and Dustin arrive home and great joy and appreciation fills me. They excitedly show me their presents from daddy-new cell phones with digital cameras. At first I feel a twinge of envy as I couldn't afford to buy them such gifts, then I remember that they are material gifts and I have also given them a gift no one can take away, and I'm sure will remain as a memory. All exhausted from our own day's events, we go to bed early.

Boxing Day is enjoyed with the welcome of Casey and Dustin's friends. I allow them to sleep over-night, to have fun and just be together with friends. Before long, conflict arises once again, this time between their friends, being a brother and sister too.

I shake my head in wonder. Why do I just manage to lift out of conflict between my children, to attract conflict among other children? A full-scale war breaks out as Casey and Dustin join in, the girls now against the boys. "Peace, peace, peace," I cry out in frustration to God, "Where is the peace, where is the love and unity?"

I get up to distract myself from the war they have created and choose some angel cards, by Doreen Virtue. The first card I pull is 'Children', the second, 'Harmony' the third, 'Spiritual growth', the fourth, 'Leadership'. The cards' messages explain I have the natural gift of working with children and that conflict is being resolved to bring peace and harmony through love. I am going through rapid spiritual growth that will impact on marriage, friends, family. I should embrace my power in a loving way and take the leadership role.

This is the perfect message of understanding for me at this time. I put away my cards and walk directly into the conflict. I order everyone to clear up and settle down, and send them off to bed. In full obedience, I am able to settle down in peace and harmony, realising that sometimes I need to be more aware of my own leadership role.

The following morning all four children want to go to Wild Waters to enjoy a day swimming in our man-made sea. I feel resistance to allowing them to go alone, but allow them to go anyway; trying my best to avoid any more conflict arising around me, as I feel drained from so many difficult lessons so close together.

I order that all their cell phones be left at home. They agree to take only their clothes and money for food during the day. Casey's friend asks to go to the mall first to draw some spending money. I drive them to the mall and wait while she goes in to draw money; she returns nervously stating that she discovered she has left her bank card at home. We go home and collect her card. I sense something is not right, but I ignore it. We return to the bank with her card, and she becomes frustrated with the machine, which will not allow her to draw any money.

Feeling sad, she manages to come up with another suggestion: to phone her mom to meet and give her money at the entrance to Wild Waters-but her cell phone is now at home.

I am truly seeing and sensing that there appears to be too many obstacles arising and we are being delayed more and more, and still I choose to ignore it.

She uses my cell phone and makes the arrangements. I deliver them to Wild Waters and leave, trying to put the obstacles out of my mind. They are left to enjoy themselves. Their dad collects them later and they come home at the agreed time.

I see how sad they are, upset and angry rather than the joyful and excited children I was expecting. Soon after arriving at Wild Waters, when Dustin and his friend were having fun swimming, their clothes, towels and money were stolen.

Casey and her friend were forced to share their money and food with their brothers. I wonder to myself how they all managed their own conflicts and feelings without parents around.

Dustin had lost two of his Christmas gifts. This teaches us that those gifts of love and memories cannot be taken away from us.

I give myself a big pat on the back for having avoided all the obstacles that attempted to prevent their day at Wild Waters. All four children were guided and taken care of through some harsh lessons in life, to learn and grow closer and be grateful for what they have. This added some value to the hidden gifts of Christmas.

Their friends apologise for all the sibling rivalry at my house, and I accept their apology and forgive them, as they say goodbye and depart with their dad.

I am pleased I have got through Christmas, and the emotions, as this I can now feel has been a huge leap forward for me.

Self-Interpretation Of Spiritual Growth

I was tuned in and aware of my feelings but was still trying to resist them at first. I experienced the power to fully surrender and allow myself to feel the hurt, experience the shifts of energy within, and be aware of the growth and lightness to come out of such experience. I also learnt how important it was to allow our children to learn their own lessons on their journey, and trust that they were never alone with all their guides taking care of them.

Is it not amazing to see how accurately the oracle angel cards related directly to my current experiences, delivering the perfect message to help me at the right time?

Chapter 27 - Birth Of The New

(Age 36, year 2005)

Expecting a peaceful New Year, it is once again not so and is instead a shake and rattle with more sibling rivalry between Casey and Dustin. They are now departing for their first full weekend stay with their dad.

My husband arrives and we, too, engage in conflict, each of us venting our anger, blame and hurt. I sit at the receiving end of hearing his point of view as the final words between us.

He feels that the past 18 years, now ending in divorce, have been a waste of his life.

At first the healer within me is grateful that my husband is actually releasing some of his anger, suppressed all these years. I try not to take this personally as I understand the driving force of anger connected to words. I would have preferred his anger directed elsewhere. I stand at the door watching the three of them driving away and feeling the huge distance between us.

I wonder if it is possible, or even necessary, to explain to him that I understand all conflicts and problems are our greatest lessons, from which we can grow, if we learn to see them as such and allow ourselves to change with them. They really are blessed gifts!

I realise how distant my husband and I had become during my spiritual growth and journey. I understand and respect the level of consciousness he is at, as I was also there some time ago in my life.

For now, perhaps it is only I who is able to find the value in the worst and best moments in our relationship. He may not be ready to see those lessons he has lived through with me in the same growing manner as I.

My thoughts are flooded with more heart-aching tears; my entire body shakes uncontrollably.

I grab a moment of fresh air and sanity outside.

It is now my time to move forward to follow my path in assisting humanity. I allow the tears and emotions to flow just as they wish while I sort through our photographs and share them out. My husband deserves his share of memories for the day when he is ready to 'take a look' at our moments together. I feel this as the end of my grieving over our divorce.

New Year's Day will bring a brand new beginning in some way. I settle down in the lounge to complete a very deep karma cleansing, working through forgiveness with a completely broken, but open, heart.

I make the conscious effort to release our marriage vows, release all my loyalty toward him. It is time to step out of this experience and move forward, especially if I intend to meet another man in the future to join me in the rest of my life's journey.

I take a long, relaxing bubble bath, enjoying all the peace and silence around me and knowing that my work feels complete in this area. I decide I really need to go to bed early as my body is weak from emotional release. I fall asleep pretty quickly, only to be woken at midnight by the loud thundering and crackling of nearby fireworks, as everyone celebrates New Year with their loved ones and friends. I notice that I no longer feel so lonely, or depressed. My grieving is over. I return to sleep peacefully and awake later to experience a wonderful miracle. A tremendous swarm of white butterflies flies right up to my window. They turn with their in-born guidance so as not to collide with the glass. They are in front of my bedroom window only.

I choose this as a sign that this year, 2005, is the dawn of success in all areas of my life. My transformation has been accomplished.

Evening arrives and I attend a Sacred Merkaba gathering linked via live teleconference from America and joined by many other countries around the world. The evening unfolds with great and powerful love and light, intense Christ-lighted energies from God. It is bliss to be with other like-minded Souls who can understand my growth and transformation and to now experience some of my rewards. Even the hugs from all who are gathered here feel so special today.

The evening closes with a sacred and special ceremony. With all the trinity healers and teachers gathered around me in a circle of love, my Master teacher leads the way and gives me the most sacred gift of healing and spiritual awakening.

I now have full understanding of the intense releases on Christmas and New Year's Eve. My preparation needed to move forward to this moment. The shift I have been feeling throughout this year heralds more change and growth ahead for 2005.

This has truly become the most powerful New Year's Day of celebration and no party with friends and family could have matched this so perfectly. I arrive home not in the least perturbed at being home alone. I climb into bed to sleep. I toss and turn but no sleep is to be had on this beautiful night. Celebration is still mine to enjoy, to have and to hold, in this moment.

My energies are so high and intense; I feel so good. I recognise that the train of thought coming through my mind presents uncontrollable written words: my prompt to continue to write my book. I sit at my computer from 11:00 pm–to 4:00 am, typing excitedly with the natural flow of words.

Self-Interpretation Of Birth Of The New

I allowed the anger being expressed to press my buttons and went all the way into feeling my own hurt still deep within me. I experienced just some of the spiritual rewards that come our way when we succeed in allowing ourselves to feel, experience and shift for the greater good of all.

Chapter 28 – Follow Your Passion

(Age 36, year 2005)

Personal Assistant VS Healer VS Writer

I begin my return journey into being a personal assistant once again at a body and mind magazine. The days begin to unfold and I sense the great difficulty of shifting back into this role. Each day brings more to light about how the skills of a personal assistant are like an 'old worn-out pair of shoes' that I am trying to fit back into. I come face to face with the other personal assistant, for another magazine in my office. I am seated opposite her. Her powerful success and beaming passion as a personal assistant beats to my own old rhythm. She loves her job. I see parts of the old me reflecting back as she mirrors certain aspects of myself. I begin feeling more and more uncomfortable as I realise how much I have truly changed. I am no longer who I was.

This is a process of showing me that I am no longer vibrating with any passion to be a personal assistant; it is purely for finances. I am strongly aware of my old, dead PA skills having faded out of me. I begin an inner dialogue with my Soul and convince myself I need to take things easy and slowly shift back into this role again for the sake of supporting my children financially. I tell myself to be gentle and loving while trying to fit back in.

Two weeks into my journey as personal assistant, my life takes a huge turn-around, guided through my body once again. Accompanied by financial and divorce stress, and my inability to trust the process of my life as a PA, this time comes to an alarming halt in my physical body.

It is Sunday evening now close to midnight. My stomach has become increasingly painful since I ate dinner. I crumple over in excruciating pain in front of the toilet. I am unable to move, the pain as great as giving birth to a baby. "What is going on?" I ask myself. I fight this process as my inner conflict begins. "I need to heal this quickly," I think, "I have to be at work tomorrow." I feel so angry with myself for creating a situation where, financially, I need to be back in the work place as a personal assistant. I am disappointed that I cannot support

170

myself and children with my work-at-home career. I feel forced to work as a PA. I am aware of a strong feeling that some parts of my Soul are nudging me and I know a huge part of me doesn't want to be there as a personal assistant. "I have to be," I tell myself in a desperate attempt to override these strong feelings of inner conflict.

"I cannot go to hospital; I have to be at work tomorrow."

I know and can feel there is a greater and urgent need for me to go to hospital. Something is just not right. I begin vomiting violently, hanging over the toilet for almost two hours. The vomiting and pain is unbearable. This is not what I want to happen; I feel the conflict of being a healer and a personal assistant tugging strongly, with an over-powering desire to become an author. For a brief moment I wonder, as a distraction: "Which career is speaking here from ego?"

Is there truly such a thing as the ego, or are we all just creating a self-sabotaging force we call an ego?" Perhaps it is just the old me in conflict with the new me. I create my own confusion in an attempt to stop vomiting.

A powerful thought of realisation comes to mind: "That we are all creating words into existence. If we don't put energy into the words we use, they won't exist."

I wonder if this is a higher dimensional sign that we need to remove some of the energies linked to some of the words in the dictionary.

My body calls for more attention and brings my thoughts back to what I need to do now. I urgently phone my mom and ask her to please take me to the hospital. We arrive at the hospital and I allow the investigations to begin. From the emergency room I am taken to the ward for admission. My doctor orders one medical test after another. Violent vomiting continues.

He refers me to the same surgeon I saw last year. She greets me and acknowledges that she remembers me. A nurse I remember from last year comes over and stands beside her. She introduces herself now as "the surgeon's personal assistant". She too remembers me from last year. Since then she has become the doctor's personal assistant. This is unbelievable, I think. Since when does a surgeon have a personal assistant? This is new to me. But it is true. Inside I laugh to myself and wonder what on earth I am supposed to see and learn from this experience.

No medication is working. Tubes are inserted via my nose into my stomach in an attempt to relieve the vomiting, but without avail.

"We have to operate," advises the surgeon. Tests clearly indicate a blocked and twisted colon. "We have to take your colon out, straighten it and put it back again." Oh no, I think. Another colon op! This can't be happening... but it is. The memories of my previous experience in intensive care are far too fresh in my mind. I relax into acceptance of the operation, knowing this will stop the vomiting.

Operation over; recovery begins. The shocking realisation of my body's actions alarms the surgeon and her PA: during recovery the vomiting continues. She researches all possible medical and scientific explanations for this. We all expected my vomiting to cease after the operation. Everything has been fixed, at least via the physical body. Of course, I am well aware I am not attending to the mind and emotions that are speaking so clearly. I resist healing myself, determined that I will ignore healing altogether as I am forcing myself back into the PA role. My own frustrations are rising strongly for having chosen to become a personal assistant again.

I am sent back to theatre to have a drip inserted into the main artery to the heart, for more filling food to be fed to me, as I am not allowed to eat or drink. I expect a full anaesthetic but to my horror discover the procedure is done using a local anaesthetic. The painful prick of the needle vibrates through my body as my tender shoulder skin is pierced. I feel warm blood trickling down my shoulder, the tube gliding into the deep artery in my body.

I shift into depression and find a way to ignore my own healing. Heavy medication helps hold me in this deep state of depression. Just to bring back my attention to healing, out of the blue my friend appears. "How did you know I was in hospital?" I ask. "Through the grape-vine," she says. She does a Reiki healing on me.

By evening I can feel my spirits lifting and my thoughts shifting out of depression and, slowly, I begin to acknowledge the real reason I am ill. Days continue with many, many tests to find the cause of my continuous vomiting. I have many opportunities to observe the surgeon and her personal assistant.

Finally, for the first time, I decide I must do healing on myself; I have to help myself, since the doctors can't. So I place my hands on the various areas of my body. I notice how my strength shifts, my thoughts change, and my inspiration lifts again. My energies are flowing high and strong from the healing. I zoom around the ward with my drip stands, exercising my body. I am repeating positive healing affirmations of acceptance. I make decisions about my future career. I choose to accept the many and various ways in which we can BE personal assistants. I am so grateful I have an income, even if I am not passionate about my job.

I am surprised with a visit from my boss; bringing me confirmation to accept just to **be** for now. She leaves a copy of our magazine for me to read.

The re-insertion of the tubes up my nose for the third time and with a thicker pipe, teaches me clearly that we should never give up. "Try and try again," are the words from my surgeon. Her PA laughs at my resistance and fear of the discomfort and pain with this procedure. "You know," she says, "most patients undergo this procedure once, but you have to have it three times. You really are brave, Tina." Her words and humour comfort me.

The puzzle pieces of my life are falling into place.

Finally, this time round, the thicker tube procedure up my nose has worked. All vomiting ceases. I recover quickly and return home.

A week later I return to work. My check-up with my surgeon confirms all is perfect. On the second day back at work, my body speaks loudly once more, just to confirm that all is not so perfect. My successfully stitched wound pops open. Blood oozes its way to the surface. I return to hospital to have it re-stitched. I know I am forcing myself to accept being a personal assistant again, purely as a means of income. Months pass with this inner career tug of war. The more I try to hide, the more the urges of creativity bubble their way to the surface. I realise how I have become a great master at suppressing myself, both to please others and for an income to survive.

Until: sharp pains vibrate across my chest, up my neck into my jaw and my left arm becomes completely numb. I feel myself losing my breath. With deep chest spasms, I feel this heart of mine wrenching tighter and tighter with each moment. Feeling dizzy, I lift my hands to my chest. I begin coughing hard and loud. Oh no, my inner healing alarm confirms my heart is trying to attack me, calling to be acknowledged. I know I have to attend to matters urgently. It is time for me to take full responsibility for my health, thoughts and feelings. No doctor present, I am in the care my own healing hands and all the assistance of the universe. This time healing is very urgent, here and now. Fortunately I am at home, but all alone-*well, kind of.* I am completely aware of my spirit healers beside me. My healing journey begins as I climb onto my healing bed. I begin carefully unwrapping my heart one layer at a time.

I see in my mind a big pretty pink bow tied tightly around my heart. I pull and untie the knot, acknowledging layers of fears and insecurities, and allow them to surface. Tears wash away ignored and suppressed areas. I continue unwrapping this beautiful heart of mine, revealing another wrapping–trust. I really need to break through the barrier of trusting myself, trusting my journey, trusting my Soul, trusting the whole universe to support me. I feel no joy in the way I am expressing myself as a personal assistant. It is time to change this. I call for joy to flood through my hands into my heart. Slowly the pain begins to subside; my chest relaxes. My dizziness clears, my arm regains some feeling. I am so tired and weak. I just rest on my healing bed and fall asleep.

I wake, knowing deep within me what to do, and it needs to be done now. It is time. I resign from my job, acknowledging I can't hide myself any longer; I must follow my heart. It is time for me to trust fully that all is in perfect, divine order.

My Soul longs to express itself through writing and healing. Days continue as I acknowledge leaping into the universe to be who I am, out of hiding and suppression, and expressing all I need to express right now.

The more I acknowledge myself as a writer and a healer, personally assisting myself and others, and all else I am, the more my creativity leaps uncontrollably, joyfully, in me.

And so it begins… my words force their way, once again, in a powerful flow into my mind, unsuppressed and ready to be written. I only need to take action. And I **do**. My thoughts guide me into the dictionary once again, my fun and joy taking over.

I acknowledge there could be a purpose for the thought of the word EGO popping into my mind just before I went into hospital. The realisation hits me loud and strong.

"All of us humans have been programmed by words in the dictionary. The energy vibration behind each word is the key. Each word is created with a letter of the alphabet. How do we know if the correct letters are being put together? Are the definitions created in the dictionary true, and if so, how do we know this?" I decide to play a little, creating my own definitions.

Oxford Dictionary: Ego – 1. *Metaphysics*. *A* conscious thinking subject. 2. *Psychol.* The part of the mind that reacts to reality and has a sense of individuality.
(My own creation) – Emotions Generating Opinions.

Oxford Dictionary: Fear – 1. An unpleasant emotion caused by exposure to danger, expectation of pain. 2. State of alarm.
(Someone else's creation) – False Emotion Appearing Real.

Oxford Dictionary: Heart – 1. A hollow muscular organ maintaining the circulation of blood by rhythmic contraction and dilation. 3. The heart regarded as the centre of thought, feeling, and emotion.

(My own creation) – Human Emotions Assisting you to Radically Transform.

Oxford Dictionary: Words – A sound or combination of sounds forming a meaningful element of speech, written or printed.

(My own creation) – Ways Of Repeating Dimensional Sounds.

Now the core of words is letters: which we use to put together a message.

Oxford Dictionary: Letter – 1. A character representing one or more of the simple or compound sounds used in speech, any of the alphabetic symbols. 3. The precise terms of a statement, the strict verbal interpretation.

(My own creation) – Language Energy Trying to Translate an Existing Reality.

Oxford Dictionary: Now – 1. At the present or mentioned time.

Instead of creating my own definition for this I choose to explain the way I see *NOW*.

We are already living in the **now**. Whether you are *presently* thinking of the past or the future, you are doing it in the **now**. Right?

You can simultaneously experience past, present and future in many different ways.

Self-Interpretation Of Follow Your Passion

My difficult return to being a personal assistant spoke very clearly to me. My hospital experience pointed out that my passion to be a personal assistant was non-existent. It also showed me the different ways in which you CAN be a personal assistant, *when you have the passion*. My Soul had now journeyed beyond, into healing, writing, feng shui, colour therapy, crystals and so much more. I had expanded beyond a PA.

In the old corporate world days, I had the EGO image of being a personal assistant. So Ego pops into mind again. There are so many aspects of myself that unfolded during this journey into personal assistant.

In the hospital I managed to accept myself in this current career by personally assisting to carry myself through to the divine moment of returning to my ability to write in a healing way.

Fortunately, I didn't allow my heart to attack me to the extent of taking a final departure from this physical body, or even a hospital visit.

I am more ALIVE than I have ever been. I truly learnt how to follow my heart and my Soul; it was speaking loudly to me.

And so it is now time to take myself into the dance of my own song of freedom. What an amazing journey I have lived.

Chapter 29 - Take Back Your Power

(Age 37, November 2005)

Oh my, once again. I have a repeated attraction calling my attention to illness and a time zone carried with it. I arrive at my doctor's rooms and ask for a bilharzia test to be done. The feelings I have within are certainly confirming bilharzia. The test results confirm that I once again have bilharzia. Fortunately, I choose to follow my intuition. I sit alone at home with the prescribed tablets in one hand and a glass of water in the other. My internal conflict speaks so loudly to me. I know the pain and suffering these tablets cause. I know I will not take these tablets. I place them back in the container and reach for a pen and paper to write my own healing script. I draw myself a golden healing worm to attract all the blood flukes and transform them into healing. I write a daily action plan for two weeks of healing. I incorporate some affirmations from Louise L. Hay with my own thoughts. I agree to release the repeated pattern of giving away my power. Days emerge with big emotional tides sweeping me off my feet in total defeat and helplessness. I surrender to the joy of experiencing my own tears washing away my hurt, my heart-ache and the many thoughts of times when I gave away my power to others. The many people I have allowed to tell me what to do and how to do it, instead of connecting with my own Soul. I almost allowed the medication to take over the healing power within me. I breathe in golden energy of peace from my Soul now, a replacement for medication, to cleanse and uplift me from the pit of depression I am in. I accept moments of defeat to exercise my ability to lift myself up again, to heal myself. A daily action of visualisation accompanies my golden healing worm inside. I guide the worm to all my organs via my blood, soothing and healing, attracting all the blood flukes for transformation. Four weeks later I decide it is time for a test to check on my progress. Finally, results give my doctor and me proof that my own healing was truly successful. I am officially free of bilharzia and, more important, a pattern has been changed. Medication was not needed. What a powerful experience!

Self-Interpretation Of Take Back Your Power

I attracted bilharzia again while on holiday in Durban, walking through a river. I truly learn here that if a pattern is not dealt with, it will repeat itself. Taking back our power may be all we need to do, especially for someone who was sexually abused as a child. As a child my power was taken from me during forced experiences. The repeated time zones when illness appears connect directly to the actual time or months it was originally created. The pure, positive power to create healing is exactly what I chose to BE doing here. I miraculously transformed my creative power and was very successful in healing myself.

Chapter 30 - New Life And New Love

(Age 37, Dec 2005 – Jan 2006)

With renewed enthusiasm after having healed myself of bilharzia, divorce, the after-effects of childhood sexual abuse and career changes, I know I have shifted and healed many patterns. I have truly grown and transformed.

I decide it is time for me to be creative and manifest the lifestyle and love of my dreams: a man who is aligned to joining me in my life. I am now ready.

To put this dream into action, I sit and write down what I would like to experience in a relationship with a man. The lifestyle we could experience together. The love I have to share with someone special. I connect to the renewed power I have within.

I choose to create this with the assistance of the whole universal team, using spirituality, feng shui, positive thoughts and powerful visualisations. I ask Archangel Chamuel to please guide this man to me as I will not be going out to look for him. One week later my cell phone delivers my manifestation. On the other end is perhaps my future love, the man of my dreams brought to reality, calling me into his life, just as I had requested. Wow! I was truly shocked at what I could create.

Two Souls united to experience life together. Joined hand to hand, body to body, eyes to eyes we lovingly dance New Year's Eve into a brand new year, a beginning for us both. Our bodies joined to dance to the music; our hearts beat to the rhythm; our Souls in complete harmony. Our love begins to grow and a journey to unfold.

Self-Interpretation Of New Life And New Love

Love. Isn't that what we all want? Yes! You can powerful co-create someone into your life to share in love. What an amazing gift to experience. Be very careful, for what you powerfully request will manifest into existence. Most of all just enjoy what you co-create, as you will certainly continue to grow from it.

Chapter 31 – Follow Your Intuition

(Age 46, Apr 2015)

I am now recently and happily married, living in a new town. I have been very healthy for the past 10 years. I choose to go for a thyroid blood test to check how balanced it is, before I begin the Banting diet to lose weight. The nurse advises that I should have a cancer screening, since my hysterectomy was a long time ago and I have not been checked since. I trust and allow her to follow her intuition and have it done. Two weeks later I receive the results. "Positive," I am told. The shock hits me hard and powerfully. This can't be happening. I already know from deep within that I will not be undergoing any chemo or radiation therapy, by my own choice. I am told to come back in three months for a follow-up test to check on the state of growth, and I will be advised further after that.

At home the shock sends powerful waves of emotion through me. I allow the tears to flow. I can't believe that cancer cells are lurking so silently within my body, giving no sign of their presence. They are in my vaginal wall. I realise how guided the nurse was to suggest the screening test. She followed her intuition.

I know better than to dwell within denial. The quicker I shift my thoughts into acceptance, the faster I can heal. So many mixed emotions arise. The healer so actively awakened within me knows the power of acceptance for healing. Three months. Hmmm. I give myself this as a healing goal. "My follow-up test will be negative, all clear," I declare to myself. I realise how many others feel when they hear such shocking news. Fortunately, as a healer, I am well aware it is only a dis-ease and not a death sentence. I know I have a choice to either view this as many do, as a disastrous journey towards struggle and possibly the end; or choose to positively heal this out of my body. Of course, you know by now which one I choose.

Yes, I know I am a powerful healer and will take this on confidently. I immediately know and am so grateful for the fact that the new diet I am on,

Banting, plays a huge role in my healing. As taught by Professor Tim Noakes of South Africa, the removal of sugar and reduction of carbohydrates in the body starves cancer cells. The introduction of fats, in particular coconut oil, heals the body in many amazing ways. I am so happy that I have now been on the diet for two weeks when I receive the "positive" results. I know I was completely guided to start this diet, which I trusted and followed through on. The diet boosts my energy levels and I feel healthier than ever. I create a healing schedule of Reiki, EFT (Emotional Freedom Techniques), positive thinking, affirmations and role playing.

My friend, Tiela, comes to visit and assists me in role playing for my healing journey. A school teacher, Tiela brings with her a powerful energy to trigger my healing and transformation.

I take myself back into my experience of childhood sexual abuse and revisit all the memories of what I thought had been completely healed and shifted. To my amazement, I spontaneously remember how I, at such a young age, found the power to put an end to the abuse. The memory of how I stopped the abuse had plagued me for some time, as I could not remember how I did it, until now. Feeling empowered with my memory I move onto the only moment that I know I have not yet dealt with, my attempt to call out for help! Time to release all the self-hatred and self-regret I accumulated for not having spoken up when I wanted to. It is time to stop punishing myself for not following through with my original intent.

In our role play, my full childhood memories unfold again: a small, young girl at school with my favourite teacher. She asks me if I would like to stay after school and help her pack all the art supplies into the cupboard. I eagerly agree as I love all the art supplies and enjoy packing things and I love being around my teacher. I feel special with this extra attention. Feeling so comfortable, I want to tell her of what is happening to me outside of school as I really hate it and have a knowingness that this is not right and I want to ask for her help. We are chatting nicely and I feel so special to be allowed to help her. I am holding a container of

182

red powder paint and decide to open it, being an inquisitive child. As I open it, she shouts, "No, Tina, the paint will fall out and cause a mess."

She grabs the container and secures the lid and places it in the cupboard. Immediately feeling bad and hating messes myself, all my feelings of not being good enough shift to the surface and I swallow hard to avoid the tears. I hate being shouted at. "I must tell her now, quickly," I think to myself. As I am about to talk she speaks first and tells me the school is closing down soon and she has loved teaching me.

"You will have to go to a new school with new teachers." The news instantly saddens me and I decide not to tell what I was about to. My calling out for help about the sexual abuse is squashed deeply as I swallow my words, hard, and hold back the tears trying to force their way to the surface.

This was the moment I shut down, too. I made my own decision to remain silent about sexual abuse and to deal with it in my own way, alone-until years later, as an adult, during my Reiki Master degree studies.

I replayed this scene of memories with Tiela, talking to her as if she were my school teacher. I tell her what happened, as if I were that little girl again. I allow the self-forgiveness, the release of hating myself for having not spoken out; and the release of the regret so deeply embedded in my body. I feel the freedom of energy rising up and releasing me completely.

My three month check-up test proves that I have successfully cleared the cancer. Dis-ease gone! Patterns cleared! I am celebrating a successful healing and it is an empowering feeling. It is now my time to move beyond old limitations and express myself freely and creatively, to continue on in life, healthily.

Self-Interpretation Of Follow Your Intuition

A nurse who was following her gut feeling and intuition is a contributing life saver. My own powerful trust in choosing to change my diet was revealed to me through this experience. If I had not started the Banting diet and decided to get my thyroid checked, I would not have known.

How appropriate that my best friend, Tiela, is a school teacher and Reiki Master to bring forth the energy required for me to role play and talk to her as if she were my teacher, as I had wanted to as a child. Tiela was able to respond to me, as a teacher and as a healer, helping me beyond my knowing at the time.

It is clearly evident here how the <u>red</u> powder paint is a triggering colour relating to the <u>root chakra</u> of our bodies governing our pubic area, the area of the body where sexual abuse took over my life. In my teacher's presence I am in a place of love, acceptance and safety to call for help, but shattering news of the school's closure overpowers my courage to talk and ask for help. My own decision to remain silent plagues my conscience my whole life, until the freedom of dealing effectively with it in Reiki and speaking openly about the experience, never to torture myself again.

"Now, you too, can heal and transform your life". – Tina Cornish

Transform Your Life

Section 2

Transforming Tools

Tool 1 - Journal

A journal is a very valuable item to have. I recommend, if you didn't have one at the beginning of this book, that you do so now before going any further. You will need it. A journal can be as simple as a writing pad or a spiral-bound note-book. It can also be a file with divisions for each type of journal you want to keep. I encourage you to find a hard-covered book, and make it special. You can create a delightful cover and colour or paint it. It is for you, so use your creativity to make this special. There are many types of journals you can have.

1. dream journal
2. healing journal
3. manifesting journal
4. gratitude journal
5. life review journal
6. art journal for creative expressions
7. meditation journal

You can create any one you like. For now we will start with a healing journal.

Tool 2 – Colourful Writing & Creative Drawing

Write colourfully in your journal. Use crayons and coloured pens. Write each sentence or paragraph in a different colour. See how you feel with the different colours. The vibration of the colours will help shift your energy. Allow yourself to draw freely and creatively. Draw squiggles, lines, and just doodle. These two, writing and drawing, will help you in your transformation. It can bring about a meditative state, a stillness, and calm. It can also trigger memories. It can awaken a child-like inspiration in you. Have fun with writing and drawing colourfully.

Tool 3 - Dreams

We all dream when we are asleep. Sometimes we do not remember them upon waking. Other times they are clear and vivid. Our dreams often give us useful information about our subconscious mind. There are also dreams that turn out to be real: the psychic and premonition dreams. Acknowledging your dreams is a truly valuable and often important process in our own healing and transformation. I highly recommend you create a separate dream journal. For further insight you may want to obtain a Dream Dictionary to help reveal the hidden messages from your subconscious.

Tool 4 - Prayer

I am sure you know what this is and how to do it already. Prayer is a simple, yet powerful conversation with your God; a time when you ask for help or give thanks for what you have. Whether you pray out loud or silently within, know both methods work. However, if you pray out loud it will carry a high, powerful, vibrational frequency. You can also write out your prayer, which has equal power.

Tool 5 - Meditation

Meditation is the time when you are silent and still; a time to receive your message of guidance from your God. I believe prayer and meditation go hand in hand. Meditation is a very valuable and important tool for a powerful transformation in your life. With regular practise you will expand your awareness greatly. Further on, I teach you how to meditate, with guided, focused meditations for you to do.

Tool 6 - Memory Recall

Memory recall often happens spontaneously. Many times there is an activity, thought or feeling that triggers a memory recall. You can also focus your attention on remembering something from your past and you will arrive within it. Memory recall is a vitally important aspect of your own healing and transformation process. Therefore, please allow yourself to go with the flow of your memories. Truly acknowledge all the feelings that come along with them. Your memories are valuable and helpful to you. Write down any memories that stand out for you. Record the feelings that you currently feel with the memory. If you have had any major traumatic experiences in your life, you may find the memories have been suppressed and forgotten about, until now. I recommend in the case of traumatic memories that you seek counsel with a near-by therapist, me, or a friend you trust. A support system is highly advantageous. I would also like to point out that you are safe while your memories surface. You have already lived through the trauma. Keep your focus on the fact it was in your past and it will not be so fearful.

Tool 7 - Faith & Trust in Divine Order

You need to have faith and trust. There is always an underlying divine order in your life. There are no 'co-incidents' as such. Everything is happening in your life for good reason and at the perfect, divine moment. Over time your faith and trust will grow as you fit together the puzzle pieces of your life and begin noticing and accepting divine order.

Tool 8 – Intuition

We all have our own in-born guidance system, our intuition. Trust it, listen to it, and follow it. It is that 'gut feeling' you get when something is out of resonance with you, a signal that something is not right; or, in resonance with you, signalling something is right. Learn to feel it.

Tool 9 – Body Talk

Talk to your body. It may sound ridiculous, but it is powerful. Ask yourself

1. How are you?

2.   Do you hurt?

3.   Where would you like attention?

4.   What can I do for you today?

Be aware of how you feel and the thoughts that come up. Acknowledge your responses.

You can draw an outline of yourself in your healing journal and mark with coloured pens what your response is from your conversation with your body. Use the same colour that may come to mind during your talk and draw it on your picture in the same place. If you don't succeed at first, keep trying and you will eventually get a response.

Tool 10 - Law Of Attraction

The law of attraction is a divine alignment of outside energy that responds to your energy. Every thought you have is immediately released into your energy field. The size and density of your thought form will depend on how much energy you have focused on it. Monitor your thoughts and words and the way you speak to yourself and others. Below is a guideline to help you remember to keep your energy in a positive space to attract the best situation for your own highest good.

1.   *What you think about you attract*

2.   *What you talk about you attract*

3.   *What you complain about you attract*

4.   *What you believe you attract*

5.   *What you fear you attract*

6.   *What you feel you attract*

7.   *Where attention goes, energy flows*

Tool 11 – Manifesting

Manifesting is all about setting and sending forth a crystal clear energy blue-print into the universe, for it to appear in your physical life. You manifest what you want in your life. You can only manifest for yourself, not for others. In your manifesting journal you can write a clear, positive description of what you want in your life and would like to experience. A lifestyle you wish for. Keep it clear, positive and in the past tense as if it is already in your life and experience. For example:

Manifesting a new car

- I love driving my new Kia Sportage
- It is orange and new
- It is easily paid off in full

Manifesting good health

- I acknowledge my body, thoughts and feelings
- I give my body the time and attention it needs to heal
- I eat healthy meals that nutritiously support my body
- I cycle regularly and love it

You can also paste in pictures of what you want. Make sure you really want that exact picture you are choosing. You can add to it whenever you like. You can regularly look at and read through your manifesting journal as this will re-inforce the imprint into your energy field for attraction. However, I also find it very powerful to just let it go and allow it to appear.

Tool 12 - Reactions

Reactions are basically our response and a change of behaviour from some kind of influence. It is our choice to react, or not, to the influence. When you understand that every person reacts at some point in their lives, you will discover how helpful this tool is in your life for transformation. This understanding will shift your level of healing into a higher dimension.

Become an observer in your life

1. Notice the reactions you have to experiences
2. Notice the way other people react toward you

When you accept reactions from people as their own, you discover this awareness. It is a vitally important tool in your life. Your understanding towards other people will shift.

Respect that each person can react in what-ever way they choose to. You do not control their reactions; you can only control your own reactions. Their choice of reactions does not have to match yours. Do not take their reactions personally. Their reactions are based on their own feelings and experiences. They are filtering the influence through their own energy field. They can also choose to change their reaction, and so can you. Ask yourself:

1. Is my reaction serving me for my highest good?
2. Is my reaction causing conflict with my beliefs?
3. What do I need to acknowledge, based on my reaction?
4. How can I change my reaction in the future?

Tool 13 - Mental Telepathy

Mental telepathy happens to all of us as some time. Have you ever known who was on the phone as it started ringing? Have you thought of someone and have that person suddenly call you? This is quite common. The more your awareness expands, the more often you will find this happening. Trust it. Allow each of those moments to build your trust and faith in using your natural, in-born skill. To work at opening it further, silently ask for someone to bring you a cup of coffee. Speak directly to them as if you were talking out loud. Then immediately let go and trust they heard you. Listen carefully to the people around you. See if you can guess what they are about to say to you. The most powerful way to enhance your mental telepathy skills is to play the game "I-spy-with-my-little-eye".

Tool 14 - Programme Your Mind

Your mind is powerful and controls your body and your life. With your mind you can reverse illness and you can also reverse aging. Have you ever considered that since the day you were born your mind has been programmed into old age. This was done by using one word – 'old'. Right from day one your parents said, my baby is one day old, two days old. Every birthday when your age changes we add to programming it further... 12 years old, 20 years old, 50 years old, etc. In fact many of us don't even wait a year to add on the next year. We say "20 going on 21". Have you ever heard anyone phrasing the age of their year-old child as, "you are one year **young?"**

Pay careful attention to the enthusiasm and celebration we experience at birthdays when we say, "You are one year **old** today". This enhances a powerful energy that is locked in a time zone and programmes our cells to continue with the aging and growing process, recording it on our DNA structure. There is scientific evidence proving new cells are continually developing and renewing. This means you have new, young cells all the time. So there is nothing stopping our programming cells into a younger age. I have been reprogramming my mind for many years now. I must say it is quite difficult to stand aside from the norm and say, "I am 46 years young". Try this when someone asks your age. You will begin to see how powerfully programmed you are to "being old" and this, too, will reflect how your mind-set can and needs to be changed to bring about different outcomes in your life. You can change your life by re-programming yourself into anything you desire. Change your thinking to positively reflect the life you desire living.

Tool 15 – EFT

EFT (Emotional Freedom Techniques) is also known as tapping. It is a technique of tapping with your fingers on the energy meridian points on your hand, face, collar bone and top of your head. The meridians of the body were first discovered by the Chinese and are used in acupressure, acupuncture and other meridian therapies. Tapping on the meridian points clears negative emotional energy blocks. It shifts your vibrational frequency and creates an open flow of energy, the result of which is emotional freedom. EFT is a rapid way to clear yourself of (unwanted) emotions, as well as mental and physical conditions, as it only takes a couple of minutes. EFT is used in a wide range of therapies for many different purposes. Many Reiki Masters combine EFT with Reiki treatments. EFT may be used in instances of illness, self-sabotage, fears, panic attacks, phobias, anxiety, grief, weight loss, cravings, headaches, and to stop smoking. The reasons are endless.

If you have suffered severe mental or emotional trauma in the past, it is highly recommended that you find a qualified EFT practitioner or therapist who can assist you through the process, as traumas resurface.

I will teach you here the basics. However, there are further learning methods with more tapping positions available on the internet. Psychological reversal and affirmations are combined with tapping. You will focus, 'acknowledge' the problem, and then use an affirmation for self-acceptance. This means you will be using a '*negative*' focus to clear yourself while you are tapping. Some examples of the phrase to use:

- Even though I have a *headache*, I deeply and completely love and accept myself.
- Even though I am *depressed*, I deeply and completely love and accept myself.
- Even though I have such *anger* towards ....., I deeply and completely love and accept myself.

- Even though I have this *craving for sweets*, I deeply and completely love and accept myself.

To tap, you will use your index and middle finger together (either hand). Tap firmly, three–to seven times, on each spot. Do not tap too hard as this will cause a bruise. Feel the level of intensity of your problem and rate it between one and ten. Repeat the phrase as you are tapping.

The tapping positions exist on both sides of the body so you can use either side, even both. The meridian positions to tap on are as follows in this order of sequence:

1. <u>Karate point:</u> on the side of your hand (either one). It is the fleshy area on the outside of the palm of your hand, used to do a karate chop. It is a tender spot to touch.
2. <u>Eyebrow beginning point:</u> just on the inside of the top of your nose.
3. <u>Side of the eye:</u> on the end of the bone bordering your eyebrow.
4. <u>Under the eye:</u> on the bone, below your pupil, in the middle point under the eye.
5. <u>Under the nose:</u> on the middle soft area between the bottom of your nose and top lip. The area that dents in.
6. <u>Under the chin:</u> midway between your bottom lip and end of chin. The area that dents in.
7. <u>Collarbone:</u> just below the collarbone. The middle area where your sternum (breast bone) and first rib meet. To find it follow the u shape bone at base of throat. Go down about 2 cm and across toward shoulder about 2 cm. It is a tender spot.
8. <u>Under the arm:</u> below the armpit in the middle where a women's bra line would be located. About 5 cm down from the armpit. It is a tender spot.
9. <u>Below the nipple:</u> just under the breast in the middle, in-line with the nipple. Where the under-skin of the breast meets the chest.
10. <u>Top of the head:</u> in the middle of the head on the top.

This is the end of the process. Now feel the level of intensity to the problem. If it is still high, repeat the tapping.

11. <u>Return to karate chop point:</u> to repeat if you desire to go deeper on clearing other thoughts that come to mind during tapping. This happens as energy shifts and you tune in more specifically to the cause of your problem.

The Puzzle of Your Life

Step 1 - Gather Your Puzzle Pieces

In your journal, write down what surfaces for you from each topic of experience as listed below. Just allow yourself to go with the flow of your thoughts, memories and feelings, in the order they appear in your mind. Do not judge them, accept what comes up for you, and let it flow naturally.

1. Your life experiences–only those that come to mind.
2. 'Co-incident' experiences.
3. Dreams you remember.
4. Moments of presence you have felt, sensed or been aware of in any way.
5. When you have been aware of thoughts that significantly shifted you unexpectedly.
6. Emotions that shifted from something you did that appeared unrelated to what you were doing.
7. Any time you have been completely aware of something happening behind the scenes of your life–divine intervention.
8. Any illnesses, even the minor ones, that come to mind and, if possible, an age with it.
9. Traumatic events and, if possible, a time or age with it.
10. Major choices or decisions you have made.

11. What keeps repeating in your life?

Step 2 - Fit Your Puzzle Together

Review all you have written. Give it time. Thoughts and memories may continue to pop up for you unexpectedly in the days that follow as you begin this process. Keep writing and adding to your experiences as they come up.

1. Ensure you record any dreams you may have following your gathering process.
2. Find your patterns and similarities in experiences.
3. Go deeper into all illnesses by using Louise L. Hay's 'Heal Your Body' book for possible causes.
4. See what links some of your experiences together.
5. Why do you feel certain things keep repeating in your life?
6. What experiences do you feel grateful for?

Step 3 - Patterns

To find and release some of your patterns, you need to review your life experiences. Write down or highlight some of the similarities you find. Ask:

1. How do you feel about your past experience now?
2. How did you deal with the event, trauma or illness?
   Now connect to your body.
3. What thought or feeling could you change?
4. Are you grateful?

Step 4 - Progression Of Healing

Healing flows through a natural process in everyone's life. Whether it is from illness or traumatic events, you will notice an automatic progression of movement through each of the seven stages below.

Accepting the process of thoughts and feelings you experience is the key to moving forward. Allowing yourself to go deeper greatly shifts your energy and consciousness, as it brings about healing.

Respect and honour your body, feelings and thoughts to help you through these stages. Give yourself time. You may not go through all these stages in one day, session or experience. You may find it occurs over weeks or even months.

7 Stages of Healing

(as taught by Barbara Ann Brennan – Light Emerging)

1. Denial
2. Anger
3. Bargaining
4. Depression
5. Acceptance
6. Rebirth (new Self emerging)
7. Creating a new life

Step 5 - Build Awareness

You can expand your awareness, by being totally open in your daily life. Interact with nature and become completely aware of your senses as you do so. Touch, smell, see, taste and listen carefully. What do all of these senses teach you? Become like a child again, learn with conscious awareness, and so heal yourself. Bring this awakening of your senses into everything you are doing daily. Walk outside on the grass, bare-foot. What do you feel? What do you hear? Listen to the birds singing every morning. Their tunes are awakening and realigning you to your day. What do you smell? You will open your awareness rapidly the more you practise using your senses. Connect with the various tones you hear from all sounds, the sensations from all touching, all the various smells and tastes. Learn to see with new eyes: see your thoughts, and see with your 'third eye' at the brow area. Remain in the present as you open your awareness and accept the gift you receive. The meditations on senses will help you further.

Step 6 - Be Open

Through an acquired state of openness you can begin to approach your life in a new way. Allow yourself new experiences as your awareness grows and expands. Do not judge them. Do not be rigid in your ways. Allow yourself to be flexible. Be aware of your new experiences. Observe your life through openness.

Step 7 - Release and Heal

The keys to taking it further, a shift out of Duality into a Unity consciousness of Oneness.

Key 1 - Forgiveness

Forgiveness is crucial to all healing. It enables you to release yourself, and others, from past events and allows you to experience healing and freedom. It is all about an energy release. I believe true forgiveness can only be achieved by going deep within. You have to work through all your feelings before you are able to shift into forgiveness. It is not about accepting that the action someone has done to you as being right but, more importantly, accepting your own feelings and releasing your energy ties to the event and the person. By retaining a rigid, and possibly narrow, view of what happened to you can only delay you from moving into total forgiveness. It is your own choice to forgive or not. Nobody can force you to forgive; you need to be truly willing and ready to do so.

Key 2 - Purpose to Forgive

My purpose was to free myself of unpleasant emotional energy and mental trauma, which was manifesting as physical illnesses, often repeating, in my life.

What is your purpose to forgive?

Focus on yourself and not the other person. Commit to do the work for yourself as first priority.

List all thoughts that come to mind:

1. List all different possibilities you think could arise through achieving forgiveness. For example, in my life it was the possibility of **freedom to be me to my fullest potential** and without the deeply hidden baggage I was carrying from the trauma of abuse.

2. List future possibilities if you choose **not** to forgive. What is your life really going to be like if you don't forgive? Will it change from what you currently experience? Who is the person to remain stuck with this energy, the thoughts, the emotions and, ultimately, the illnesses? Yes, it would be You.

Key 3 - Acceptance

Accept past events as they are. It is impossible to change the events that have already taken place. Yet know that you can change your attitude towards past events.

Allow yourself to go deep into your own emotions. You now have the opportunity to see the events in a different way and to begin changing your attitude.

By taking acceptance into the past with a new view opens many different possibilities in life. It is empowering and very healing to go back into the past and review all the areas in your life that were affected, and accept the way you chose to handle it at the time.

Go back with a different and positive view on those times. In my own experience I quickly saw a pattern that I had not recognised. I saw my own powerful and unique way of handling trauma awakening me to what we all have within us: the strength and inner knowing to overcome whatever we experience in our lives.

You will see your own pattern and find your power and strength, too. With a different attitude your past can become very empowering for you. I encourage you to allow yourself to experience this.

Key 4 - Gratitude

Accepting and changing your perspective of the event can help incredibly. But to find a way to be grateful for the gifts and wisdom the experience may have opened for you transcends and brings your healing to a whole new level. You will discover there are many different ways of viewing a past experience. We all have our unique ways, born within us, to overcome trauma.

1. What are you grateful for in each circumstance?
2. What aspects of yourself came up and out from the experience?
3. How empowering is it to find gratitude?

Key 5 – Purpose of our Souls

I believe we choose before birth to experience certain events in our life. We all have a purpose to love, to give-and to serve. There is a purpose for all your experiences. How we deal with these events is our own choice. If you can allow yourself the peacefulness to trust in your Soul and God's divine order, you will be open to the higher reality that your traumatic experience was for your own divine and highest good. You can then see your life unfolding toward your own highest potential, and empowering you towards your fullest divine Soul expression in this life.

Key 6 – Cleansing through Love

After working through all these keys above, close your eyes for a while. Go within and connect to God and your Soul and ask for, and then accept, a complete cleansing of forgiveness through love and light. Feel this love and light flush out and cleanse any remaining cords and energy spots of un-forgiveness still present within your energy field and cells in your physical body. Trust that they will be replaced with divine love and healing light. A cleansing meditation is further on.

Key 7 – Judgements

Every one of us has judged ourselves, or another, at some time in our lives. Releasing judgements and criticisms are ultimately the highest key to moving into a unity consciousness of oneness. This, too, is necessary for healing oneself completely. Releasing judgements can be just as difficult as forgiveness, if not more so. I encourage you to use and follow through with my same the steps as in forgiveness, and apply this to all judgements you may have *towards yourself and others*. One big question is: whom are you holding back by not choosing to move through this step? Who feels the pain? Naturally, the answer would be YOU. Just as in forgiveness, your feelings and emotional connections are what truly need to be worked through to achieve this release. Only you can move yourself through this doorway. I believe we judge only because we see ourselves as separate from others, and not as one.

1. What is your purpose in judging?
2. What is your desire in changing this?
3. Accept that you do judge, and have done so in the past. You have also judged your own experiences.
4. What could the Soul purpose be in judging ourselves and others?
5. Cleanse yourself of judgement with forgiveness. In other words, forgive yourself for judging.
6. Gratitude is the key here. The more you are grateful for-and truly appreciate-all that you have, all that you do, all that you are-and apply the same to others, the more powerfully you will open the 'eyes within your heart'. You will experience a release of judgements as you move into your own divine energy. Gratitude is the best way to empower and

heal yourself. Allow yourself to feel it, share it and receive it. Be grateful for all the people and experiences in your life.

7. Re-create oneness through love. To do this: love yourself for what you do and bring to others; and love others for what they do and bring to your life.

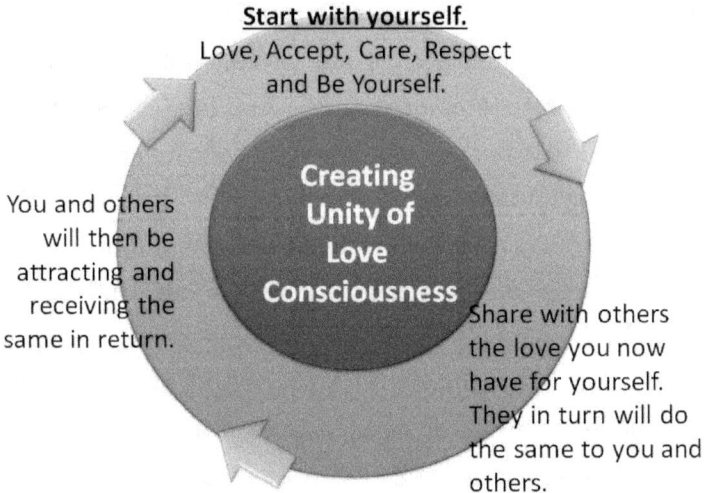

Image 9 – Creating Unity

Step 8 - Find Out Who You Are

To Become WHO YOU ARE and release WHO YOU ARE NOT

To become centred and focused on yourself, sit for a second or two with your eyes closed. Take a deep breath. Now, while remaining in-touch with yourself, open your eyes and read out-loud the list below of 'positive' Soul characteristics. Do this daily.

Be aware of any feelings of resistance or disagreement. Write down in your journal any characteristic where you feel resistance. This will give you a quick and accurate indication of blockages you have within yourself, based on your own opinion of yourself and/or the influence of others' opinions.

The blockages need your acceptance. This list is just a guideline to all you truly are at Soul level; the positive aspects of yourself. You will be able to identify what you need to integrate with, or more importantly, remember from Soul, that you are completely whole, magnificent and unique.

This is where we begin to realise that we are all truly already one and in unity at a Soul level. Knowing this helps you to forgive and let go of judging others in the future and those from your past. You will then naturally shift yourself from a dual perspective or reality, to one of unity-oneness.

"Being all of who you are is truly all you need to be." Tina Cornish

Soul Characteristics – Positive List

I, (insert your name)   , AM all of this and more....

I am fun	I am courageous	I am supporting
I am loving	I am forever growing	I am tolerant
I am joyful	I am honest	I am insightful
I am peaceful	I am forever learning	I am beautiful
I am open	I am fulfilled	I am free
I am fit	I am creative	I am unconditional
I am truthful	I am forgiving	I am universal
I am balanced	I am powerful	I am unique
I am empathic	I am respectful	I am angelic
I am accepting	I am happy	I am self-disciplined
I am understanding	I am successful	I am miraculous
I am optimistic	I am spontaneous	I am gifted
I am positive	I am nurturing	I am wise
I am exciting	I am harmonious	I am spiritual
I am compassionate	I am worthy	I am reliable
I am relaxed	I am abundant	I am bright
I am giving	I am aware	I am young
I am intelligent	I am internally strong	I am remembering
I am energetic	I am calm	I am multi-skilled
I am special	I am safe and protected	I am determined
I am enduring	I am blessed	I am amazing
I am human	I am experiencing	I am divine
I am truthful	I am changeable	I am helpful
I am playful	I am rich	I am conscious
I am healthy	I am prosperous	I am wonderful
I am sincere	I am wealthy	I am healing

I am sexy

I am romantic

I am warm

I am grateful

I am light

I am psychic

I am clairvoyant

I am clairaudient

I am claircognisant

I am clairsentient

I am thoughtful

And more. (list anything else you know you are)

I am all that I am

Your uniqueness, of course, will shine through when you really feel and/or know that you are already any and all of these qualities in abundance, and you bring these to your everyday life and skills so naturally.

1. Look at those characteristics you wrote down to which you hold a resistance, e.g. you may feel, I am *not* beautiful.

2. Clearly identify which of these are your own, true, feelings about yourself, or have you been influenced by what others have said or made you feel in the past? e.g. *someone may have told you* that you are not beautiful.

3. Work first on the feelings driven by others. Understand that these feelings are based on others' opinions that have influenced you. You have absorbed and accepted these opinions or, more accurately, already have them actively reflecting an energy field.

4. Are they currently an influence in your life? e.g. do you still believe you are not beautiful?

5. Agree with yourself to release all of these opinions of *whom you are not* and allow yourself to become all of *who you are*. When you identify past actions that matched these characteristics, you may find yourself believing them to be true. e.g. you look in the mirror and now fully believe you are not beautiful.

6. This, again, is your opinion of **what you are not.** This clearly identifies for you that an energy connection remains within you to one of your past actions or thoughts related to an event.

7. Identify what you learnt or can now learn from this event (when someone told you, you were not beautiful) and then release it. A quick releasing method is to step out of denial and acknowledge a lesson is to be learnt. You attracted this for a purpose. Allow any emotion out, whether it is anger, hurt or whatever it is. Use EFT to clear. Imagine yourself releasing to God or the universe, whoever you choose. Don't hold onto it. Move on to allowing yourself to fully accept that which **you truly are**. e.g. you are beautiful.

8. By reading the full Soul characteristic 'positive' list to yourself daily and working through your resistance, you will begin to notice the changes you can make within yourself and radiate out into your life. Don't give up on yourself.

9. Now let us take this one step further to dissolve any judgement you may still have upon others, by remembering all of **who you truly are** is also all of which **others** truly are. This is oneness–unity. The greatest transformation here is to discover you are everything already. This is also what I believe to be 'love consciousness'.

Step 9 – Express Your Soul

Now that you know who you are, let us discover your expression. Where in your life do you express your Soul? Using the above Soul Characteristics Positive List, go through the list placing a small 'h' for home, a small 'c' for career, a small 's' for socialising, a small 'w' for worshipping.

This exercise could indicate areas that you need to integrate, or in which you need to accept more of yourself, to bring about balance in your life and thereby express all of **YOU** in all of **your** life. For example: you may feel you are successful in your career but not at home. Then ask yourself the following.

1. Why do you feel you are not successful at home?
2. Accept it and release it. Change your thoughts and feelings and beliefs. You are the only one who can make this shift and change. This is your life and you get to choose your expression.
3. What do you do at *home* that you can see and feel as your *success*?
4. What can you do differently at *home* to bring about the *success* you would like?
5. How will you recognise when you are *successful* at *home*?

Step 10 – Align to your Life Purpose

All of our purposes reflect loving, giving and serving in some way. The exercises that follow will help you gain more awareness on aligning to your life purpose. I prefer to use the word align here, not 'find'. This is because your life purpose is not lost and needing you to find it, but more accurately it is within you already and only needs you to align with it. This means to recognise it, be aware of it, accept it and take action if you are not already doing so. I also refer to a Life Purpose being about your career and/or a relationship, even many relationships. You have come to earth to love, give and serve in and through a unique expression that only you can fulfil. For some, your purpose could be to be a mother or a father, a wife or a husband, and have no career as such. For some it involves a career and being in relationships with others.

So therefore these exercises can be applied to both 'career' and 'relationships'. You choose which you would like to work on. You can also work on them all. Careers involve relationships, so this task does not only apply to a relationship with a spouse or family member. There are many relationships you have. Relationships are powerful in the fact that they mirror some of your own Soul uniqueness.

I would suggest that if you are going to work on both, then ensure you have separate headings for Career / Relationships on all your working lists. If working on multiple relationships, then also ensure you use that person's name as a heading.

List 1 - Skills

Make a list in your journal of all the skills, knowledge, qualifications and experience you have from your past and current career/relationships. Be sure to include that which you have gained through hobbies and recreational activities, and anything you were truly good at in school. Connect to anything that you really feel good doing.

List 2 - Why YOU do this

Be very honest with yourself and list the reasons you are doing what you are doing, and what you have done in the past. Some questions to ask yourself:

1. Are you in a career your parents wanted for themselves, or for you?
2. Did you just, somehow, end up in this career?
3. Are you doing this because you WANT to do it?
4. Are you only doing this for money?
5. Are you in this relationship because you WANT to be?

6. Are you in this relationship because others want you to be?

7. Are you truly HAPPY doing what you are doing?

8. Are you truly HAPPY with this relationship?

9. Then ask yourself if you have the DESIRE to BE this person.

List 3 – Learning

Understand that whatever you are doing or have done, you are always aligned with your Soul/life purpose. You will gain something you need to learn or build strength in and that is required for your full Soul expression. We often hear people say, "I was in the WRONG career and/or relationship". This means, more appropriately, that there was/is a far greater purpose for you, and always is. 'Wrong' is not necessarily bad, it just means you were not able to **express** all of YOU in this area. As you expand into more of yourself, you outgrow careers and/or relationships. You will feel a 'pulling you away' from **WHO YOU ARE** (your Soul/life purpose or expression). Most of you will feel this nagging pull in your stomach/solar plexus area of your body. The moment you decide to, and start to, align, you will feel the release in your body. Not all of us need to change careers/relationships. Many are aligned, or have chosen the 'correct' career/relationship to express their full Soul purpose throughout life. You are gaining experience, you are always learning. Often the other aspects of your Soul can be expressed in recreational areas outside of your chosen career. Make a list of:

1. What have you learnt from your current and past careers/relationships?

2. What kinds of values and characteristics have been built and strengthened within you?

3. What do you still want to learn?

4. What do you feel so attracted to?

List 4 - Something Different

Make another list of all the different thoughts you have had about doing something different in your life. Especially include any 'gut feelings' you have had recently. Be sure not to let any fears and perceptions of inferiority prevent you from writing **all you need** to write down. Ask yourself: what would YOU be happy doing, be passionate about doing and be inspired about doing. Express yourself as fully as you can.

List 5 - What YOU Enjoy

Go back to the skills list that you have gained from your past. Circle any that you really enjoy doing and wish to continue doing. Remember to include any hobbies or recreational activities.

List 6 - Characteristics

Now use the list of WHO YOU TRULY ARE, the positive Soul characteristics from step 8.

1. Select the characteristics required to do all you have done in the past, including your qualities that shine through.
2. Then fit those characteristics to what you may be required to do on each of those on your lists: 4 (something different) and 5 (what you enjoy).
3. Remember WHO YOU ARE and express it.

List 7 - Create YOUR life

Based on the awareness you now have, write down what you truly feel you could be doing. Do not let any fears or perceptions of inferiority stand in your way. Be open and inventive in creating your own profession, career or relationship, should there not be one in existence. Listen to your gut. It will guide you. Your Soul already knows and is speaking to you.

List 8 - YOUR Fears and Inferiority

If 'Creating your Life' just brought up some fears and feelings of inferiority in you, you will need to work on it further. Your thoughts and feelings are stumbling blocks, perhaps self-sabotage and, more importantly, they are giving you the opportunity to clear them. Go wild and list all these stumbling blocks in your life. You may even feel so strongly about some profession that requires a high qualification and you may *think* you are too old, or not intelligent enough or otherwise insufficiently capable to study this now. Be completely aware that these stumbling blocks, feelings and thoughts are possibly an indication of your own opinions about yourself, based on what others may have said to you in childhood/past. Pay careful attention to anything that comes to mind that could originally have been said to you in your life. This could have come from parents, siblings, relatives, teachers, friends, spouses-anyone. Understand that these people may have always meant well when they said it to you, but it was based on their own opinions, fears and inferiority. They, too, are as human as you are. This is the most important list. It requires healing and releasing of any negative thought patterns and blocks created in you and the emotional ties you have to these. Take full ownership of these feelings, even if they were the result of influences upon you. It is YOU who now sits with these feelings; you are the only one who can change the way you think and feel. By releasing these, you can move forward with absolute courage and confidence to succeed in whatever you desire to BE. If you move forward into something new, without healing through this list, you may create that which you fear the most. You will carry an energy attraction pattern in your vibration. If this happens you must realise that it is YOUR fear or inferiority pattern that is being highlighted for your attention, and it requires healing. It does not mean you are a failure. If you happen to think you have failed, I am sure you have heard that "failures are your best learning opportunities". You are learning, experiencing and shifting. You are never too old to change or learn and study a new profession and gain the qualifications or direction you may require. Remember we are all multi-skilled Souls and need only apply all of ourselves in our careers/relationships. To release this list and the energy of the feelings, you can do any of the following:

1. Write out the list on a piece of paper and burn it, saying "I release these fears now".

2. Write out the list on another separate piece of paper and tear it up into the bin, saying "I release these fears now".

3. Write out the list on another separate piece of paper and tear it up in small pieces and throw it into a fast moving river, saying "I release these fears now".

4. Do a meditation and visualise these fears floating out of you, up into a cloud. It could be a balloon with a string. As you let go the string, say "I release these fears now".

5. Pray for a cleansing and releasing of these fears now.

6. Use EFT (emotional freedom techniques).

Now you need to replace those fears you have released with positive feelings you wish to have; those that are already within you, waiting for you to acknowledge and accept them fully. Refer to your positive Soul characteristics list for help. In this way you will re-programme your mind into a positive state, helping you to align with your purpose and move toward experiencing it.

You may or may not know at this stage exactly what it is that you need to do, even after doing all these exercises. This is okay. It is also an indication of a missing piece of your puzzle, the connection to your Soul. Allow yourself to connect with your own Soul. This can sometimes be difficult to accomplish and I would encourage you not to force yourself, get frustrated, or perhaps even give-up. More importantly, you need only to **trust** yourself that you will KNOW what you need to do, and when you need to do it. Divine timing is important with this exercise, as there may still be far more you need to learn and experience or become aware of. I can only encourage you to keep at it, as you will be able to accomplish this connection and *know* what you need to do. The following sections of my book on Spirit Guides and Meditation can and will assist you further with this exercise if you are having difficulties connecting with your Soul.

Sit still, with focus and intent to connect to your Soul. Do not be concerned where you will find your Soul. Some find it outside of themselves; some find it in the solar plexus or heart area of their bodies. Just *trust* that wherever it is, you will connect to it. What is important is the information you receive, not where your Soul is. You will receive this information through thoughts and ideas, feelings and even external signs. You need to ask yourself, out-loud or inwardly, "What do I need to *BE* doing, to *BE* all that I am in this life?" Then just sit, relax, meditate and question your guides and your God for further assistance. Be quiet and listen. See, sense and feel the answer coming to you.

Full trust and faith will connect you to your Soul. The more you practice this connection, the stronger it will become and more information will come to you.   Write down everything, even if it does not make any sense right now.

1.   What were the feelings?
2.   What were the ideas?

A meditation to connect with your guides and guardian angels is to be found later in these pages, as is a meditation to connect with your Soul.

Step 11 - Beliefs

Beliefs are very powerful influences in our lives.   It is wise to become aware of the beliefs that are currently playing a role in your life. If possible, change some of your beliefs to serve your highest good.

1.   What are my beliefs?
2.   How are my beliefs influencing my life?
3.   Are my beliefs serving me for my highest good?
4.   Are these beliefs my own or influenced by someone else?
5.   How can I change my beliefs?
6.   Do I have a different belief within me?
7.   How will changing my beliefs change my life?

Step 12 - Balance Your Life

Now you need to empower your life into the future. To begin with, we need to establish how balanced your life is right now. This is a useful technique to self-assess your life at this current moment. Create a Life Cycle, formed by 8 segments of your life.

1.   Spirituality
2.   Home & Family
3.   Fun & Leisure
4.   Career

5. Finances
6. Relationships & Communication
7. Health & Fitness
8. Self-Development

In your journal draw a circle as below, divided into 8 segments. Write next to each of these segments the 8 areas of your life. Use coloured pens. In any order, but don't copy the order as listed. It is vitally important to jump around and place them in any area, as the desire takes you. Be sure to put a date at the top of this Life Cycle. This is important. You will want to refer to it later in your life when you repeat this exercise.

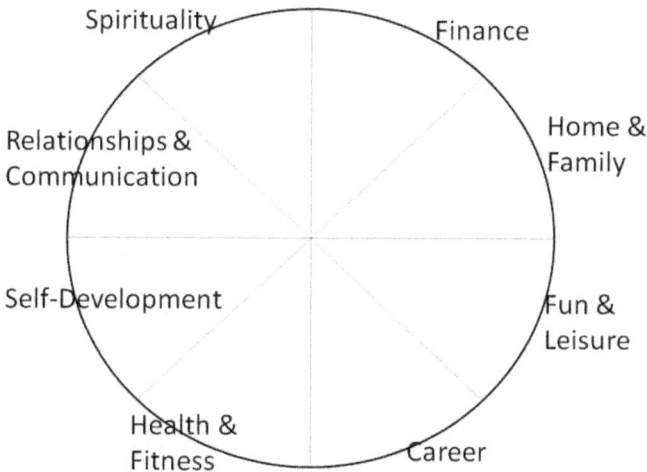

Image 10 – Segmented Circle

Colour-in each segment, showing an estimate of the percentage of balance you feel you are maintaining in your life at the moment. Each segment is divided into 10 portions.

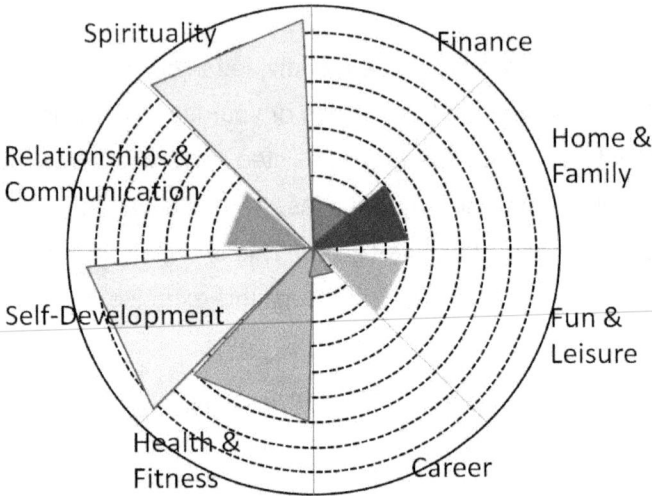

Image 11 – Coloured Cycle

Example

This reveals to you an interesting estimation of your life. Take a look at the topics opposite one another. For example, Health & Fitness at 60% opposite Finance, at 20%. You will be able to relate to the fact that Health & Fitness is consuming more of your energy than Finance. And so on. Look at how your own Life Cycle reflects those areas where more energy is being spent. Write down suggestions as to how you can bring this into balance by spending more time in any areas reflecting at a low percentage. Questions to ask yourself:

1. What can I do to give more attention to....?
2. What can I change to create more time for attention on....?
3. What am I resisting?

4. Why does this feel so out of balance?
5. What are my fears?
6. If I knew how to change this, what would the solution be?
7. What could I give up from … (segment) to focus more energy on (segment)…?
8. Set, and write down, a goal to make this change.

Repeat this Life Cycle about every six months and you will begin to see how you are balancing your life. You will notice how your life is transforming. When you repeat it, do not look back at your past exercises. You do not want to copy the order of placement of the segments. After completing the exercise you can compare it to a previous one. Notice how your life shifts and transforms.

Step 13 - Spirit Guides & Guardian Angels

We all have our own spirit guides and guardian angels to help us in life. Everyone can communicate with their guides and angels, even the archangels, just as easily as you can with your God.

You will have your own, strong sense of contact with guides. This can be:
1. seeing visual apparitions
2. mentally seeing pictures or visions
3. feeling a change of energy around you
4. smelling a fragrance
5. hearing a high-pitched energy vibration
6. hearing audible words
7. receiving messages through thoughts and ideas.

Be open to any one or more of these forms of communication with your guides. Understand that your guides are never present to scare or harm you in any way. They are highly trained beings who totally respect and guide you, in accordance with your own Soul.

It is common to see and/or feel, or obtain a name for a spirit guide who is present during a meditation, dream state or awake mentally. By simply asking with positive intent, your request is met. It is important to trust your own first instincts when encountering your guides for the first time.

Spirit guides are most often seen in some way once we uplift our energy vibrations to meet theirs.   Our energy vibrates at different frequencies and becomes considerably lighter and higher during meditation. Meditation is not absolutely necessary to be in contact with your guides but does enhance your ability.

Spiritual blocks, as they are often called, are created through fears, self-doubts, insecurities, tensions and mind chatter from our own thoughts. Forcing yourself to try to see your guides will bring pressure to bear, thereby lowering your vibrations and decreasing your chances of consciously meeting them.

Do not be discouraged if, when you make requests of your guides for help, they do not *appear* to be granted. There are many important reasons why this can *appear* to be the case.

Firstly, your requests have to meet with your Soul contract. Secondly, your requests must not be with the intention of manipulating or controlling others. Do not place limitations on your requests. Sometimes they are granted and delivered in unexpected ways that are appropriately aligned with your Soul. Divine timing also plays an important role. This means there are sometimes important parts of your life that must fall into place before a request can be met. Be assured and trust that the celestial realm does hear and answer your requests at all times in the best possible way for you.

A meditation to connect with your guides and guardian angels is further on.

Step 14 - Archangels

Archangels exist as the mighty helpers of God who supervise guardian angels, angels and spirit guides. There are many archangels with various duties and assignments for helping all of creation shift and ascend. If you want powerful and immediate assistance, you can call upon an archangel. They are pure spiritual beings who vibrate at a very high light and colour frequency, higher than that of our guardian angels and spirit guides. They have no restriction to geographical location and can be present in multiple spaces. Because of the "law of free will" we need constantly to invite them into our lives, as they will never intervene unless there is a life-threatening situation. However, because of their high vibrational frequency, the moment you call, they are with you instantly. To have a clearer two-way connection and communication with archangels, you need to shift your vibrational frequency into a higher and lighter state. To do this, you need to be in a state of gratitude at all times. By releasing physical blocks, anger, emotional baggage, judgements and negativity, you free yourself of static dense vibrations. This will shift you into a gratitude state where you can easily exercise forgiveness frequently. By continuing to purify your frequency, you will enhance your communication and connections to the archangels without distortion. This does not mean they will not help you if you are in a negative vibration when you ask for help. It does mean you will most likely not **be aware** of their presence. Your senses need to be alert and aware for you to know they are with you.

Physical blockages are caused by a high intake of sugary foods, fizzy drinks, chocolates, coffee, smoking, alcohol, medications, drugs and toxins. It is wise to wean yourself from these as much as possible. Do not stressfully force yourself to wean, but rather ask the archangels to guide and help you to do this. Normally the most abusive to your body will be the first things you will be guided to focus on.

Purifying your home or area of regular communication with the archangels is also an advantage. Our homes and environment absorb negative energy just as easily as we do. Open windows and curtains to allow the air and light to circulate around your home. Clearing clutter will greatly uplift the energies in your home and, as a result, affect your own energies positively. Areas of your home that attract arguments and fears on a regular basis are a sign of stagnant, negative energy in need of clearing. You can also clear the area with music, burning incense or aromatherapy oils, or spraying a delightful fragrance into the air.

Expect to be surprised when you begin working with archangels. Sometimes your requests are fulfilled before you even finish asking for their help.

You can connect with any of the archangels listed below.

Archangel Michael – deep to royal blue with purple-red sparkles

- Call for protection, physically, emotionally, and psychically.
- Cut relationship cords.
- Need confidence, courage and motivation for any situation.
- Align with your life purpose.

- Remove your fears.
- Stand in your own power and tell the truth.
- Mechanical and electrical assistance, even with computers.
- Sacred geometry understanding.
- Guide leaders in government truthfully.

Archangel Jophiel - yellow

- If you need mental clarity and wisdom in any way; when you are studying for exams, to understand and retain information.
- Releasing thought patterns associated with addictions from chocolate, nicotine to alcohol.
- Assists all teachers to bring forward knowledge and wisdom.
- If you are spring-cleaning, clearing clutter and re-decorating.
- Help in picking up new skills required for your Soul purpose.
- Need inspiration, joy, laughter and beautiful thoughts in your life.
- Art and creative projects.
- Exposes wrong-doing in government and businesses.

Archangel Chamuel – deep pink

- Be uplifted from sorrow; depression; hopeless, low self-esteem; and loneliness.
- Loving yourself and others. To feel compassion and empathy.
- Let go of being judgemental and critical.
- Difficulties in relationships. Renew relationships with more love and compassion.

- If you need to find something you have lost, or can't remember where you left it; find a new house; find a suitable job more aligned with your Soul purpose; find your Soulmate.
- Shift humanity into a unity of love consciousness.

Archangel Gabriel - white

- Realign to your Soul purpose and career. Understand more about what your life purpose is and what steps you need to take. Starting a new business. All legal and business pursuits.
- Assistance in the communication arts, creative expression such as writing, speaking, delivery of news. Help in putting across your teachings to help others.
- Helps you to take leadership with the knowledge gained and the way in which you share it with others.
- Difficulties in parenting and family. Establishing a new relationship or repairing an old one.
- Interpreting your dreams and gaining direction or teachings through them.
- Cleansing impure thoughts that are interfering with your Soul purpose and body purification by releasing toxins.
- If you require more joy and direction and help prioritising your obligations and goals.
- Relief for victims of natural disasters. Distribution of food and medical supplies. Bringing about peace.

Archangel Raphael - green

- Assists in all forms of healing–: body, mind, spirit and Soul. Assists doctors, nurses, health practitioners, everyone involved in healing others.
- Healing animals, finding lost animals.
- Healing yourself. Ask to be guided into eating and drinking what is healthy for you. Best exercise programme or sport suited for you and your purpose. Releasing patterns of attraction for illness you may experience, moving you into healthier attitudes and experiences.
- If you are undergoing surgery or treatment.
- Assist with medical and scientific studies, skills and new cures.
- If you need to bring unity into your life and need to feel more whole. Uniting various nations together.
- Release from poverty consciousness into abundance consciousness. Receiving wealth. Food, clothing, shelter, tools of trade, anything.
- Releasing you from believing in superstitions. Improve clairvoyance.

Archangel Uriel – deep gold with purple, blue and ruby flecks

- Need to find inner peace. Peace in your home, family and environment. Releasing you from inner turmoil. Clearing up disagreements, removing problems at work and in relationships. Releasing past burdens and hurt.

- Help in your psychological behaviour. Healing emotional turbulence and the patterns that create it.
- Removing anger, frustration, irritation and violence, etc.
- If you have difficulty in receiving and accepting.
- If you want to be 'in service to others' and need guidance on this.
- To fill you with a renewal of hope after disappointments.
- Inspiration for nurses, doctors, hospice workers, counsellors, teachers, judges, public servants and all who serve others. Peace and understanding to help end war.
- Help in earth changes and natural disasters.

Archangel Zadkiel – deep violet-purple

- Forgive yourself and others for healing.
- Remove all negativity from your life and transform it into positive energy. Release from limiting behaviours. Keep yourself aligned in positive behaviour that serves you.
- Purify your body, mind and Soul. Cut cords with others. Release negative karmic cords to past actions.
- Transmute spiritual energy and help in absorbing it.
- Joy, lightness, hope and newness of life.
- Release emotional connection to painful memories.

Focused Meditations

Meditation is an exercise of the mind. It is your own, natural ability to mentally focus and visualise something. Meditation is practiced world-wide for many different purposes. Meditation is often used as:

1. a relaxation and stress-release method
2. mental clarity and understanding
3. healing the body
4. connecting with God
5. connecting with Soul
6. connecting with angels, guides, the celestial realm
7. being creative
8. enhancing self-development
9. opening and expanding awareness
10. problem-solving.

Everyone meditates at some point in life. Our own simple daydreams are meditations. A simple, focused interaction with nature is meditation. Have you ever stared out of a window, watched the rain falling and become completely mesmerised? Have you ever stared into the flames of a fire and become completely drawn in? These are short and brief moments of meditation. Any mental focus where you are totally absorbed in what you are doing and 'at one' with yourself is a meditation. Meditation is born within each and every one of us. I want to bring you the simplicity of meditation, as well as the most effective way for you to drop any fears and negative beliefs you may have about meditating. Do not latch onto fears of meditation and restrict yourself from experiencing this wonderful exercise.

I give you techniques to provide deeper focus in the meditation to enhance your experience and maintain the true meditative state (theta) for longer. Theta is the natural brain-wave state that we all experience as we fall asleep and as we wake up. In beta brain-wave, you are awake, alert and concentrating. In alpha brain-wave, you are calm and relaxed. Theta is the next state, a meditative state, deeply creative. You pass through this brain-wave quite quickly as you go to sleep. Delta brain-wave is a deep sleep state.

In theta, the left and right sides of your brain vibrate together. Theta is the state in which you are able to spontaneously remember the previous night's dream, just before going to sleep. With time and practice in meditation, you will be able to keep yourself in theta brain-wave for longer than when you go to sleep.

What you will learn here are the basic techniques and steps to follow for a more focused meditation. There are many and varied meditations to follow; however, I believe your very best meditation will come from within you, from your own mind, relating directly to your own unique needs. Although I am going to share some of my own meditations with you, I encourage you to stretch your own creativity and allow yourself to divert into the mental focus that emerges naturally for you. By doing this, you will acknowledge your own powerful and unique healing abilities.

Meditation is a perfect tool or vehicle through which you can achieve and grow more in your life. You can do it alone or in a group. Group meditations do bring an increase in powerful energies and focus as many gather together. Usually your meditation becomes stronger, with much more clarity, in a group.

Step 1 – Stretching

Stretching is an excellent way to realign your energies both before and after your meditations. Before meditation, it stretches your muscles, which prepares them for easier relaxation. After meditation, stretching helps to align all of your energy bodies (spiritual, astral, mental, emotional and physical) and helps bring back your focus to the present. You can stretch while sitting or, if you prefer, standing. Try both and find which you are most comfortable with.

Step 2 – Posture

Beginners should always sit in meditation, to prevent falling asleep. Remember meditation (theta) state is the natural brain-wave that you are used to going through quickly to fall asleep at night. It is more comfortable to sit in a chair. Advanced meditators have usually practiced and have developed their back and core muscles to support themselves comfortably when sitting on the floor without back support. A comfortable chair is perfect.

Keep your back straight, uncrossed feet comfortably on the floor and arms comfortably at your sides, palms facing up.

Step 3 – Intention

Always set your intention for meditating. This helps guide your energy and increases your ability to focus. You can hold to the intent being that your mind becomes still when you start and your awareness opens up. Or your intent can be of receiving healing. It is your choice.

Step 4 – Grounding

Grounding is an important visual technique, used to connect all your energies to the space you are in and extending into the core of the earth. This helps to prevent a potential energy overdose (mentioned below). You quite simply imagine roots of energy extended or growing out of the soles of your feet through to the core of the earth. I imagine the core of the earth as a rose quartz crystal as a technique to lovingly balance the higher energies being absorbed during meditation.

Step 5 – Breathing

This may seem inappropriate as we are always breathing. Some choose to ignore breathing techniques, but I like to focus on it for a good reason–it enhances my meditation and helps me to relax. At times we are not even aware of our breathing habits. Are you breathing effectively? Is it just a shallow breath using only a small part of your lungs? Stress, posture or respiratory disorders can often influence breathing habits. There is an easy way to fix this. Commit to focusing on your breathing every hour during the day for one week. Spend just one minute watching how you are breathing. Breathing is vital to bring in more oxygen and energy. Then focus on changing your breathing in that one minute. Allow it to become deep and controlled. Deep breathing will automatically slow down the activity in your brain, reduce stress, encourage relaxation and enhance your ability to focus in your meditation. When starting your meditation, allow yourself time to focus on deep breathing. You will notice immediate changes in your body. Focused breathing is often used in meditation as both a calm-down and a wake-up technique. Different deep breathing techniques are used by advanced meditators to increase energy flow. Therefore, it is important to note that when you start to meditate, you should only take on short ones, of about 10 to 20 minutes. Gradually increase your time as you develop your level of vibration. Meditations longer than 30 minutes to begin with could cause you to experience an energy overdose. This is because when you meditate you absorb higher vibrational levels of energy, a much purer frequency than you may be accustomed to, especially if you live a highly stressful life. An energy overdose is recognised by irritability, nervousness, dizziness, light-headedness, feeling 'spacey', as well as nauseous. You might also develop a headache directly after your meditation. If this should happen, you can easily fix it through closing your eyes again and focusing on breathing, re-grounding and mentally accepting the higher frequencies you absorbed.

Step 6 – Spiritual Hygiene

You need to clear any fears you may have of meditating. These usually relate to fear of having one's mind influenced or body taken over by 'evil entities' beyond one's control. Usually these fears are a result of religious teachings or of hearing of bad experiences from other people. Be careful not to allow other people's experiences to interfere with your life.

Spiritual beings, especially our own guides, are with us at all times, not just during meditation.

I place the 'evil entities' into the category of negative beings. I believe that just as there are sometimes negative humans trying to control and manipulate others, so too are there negative beings in the spiritual realm. We are all various frequencies of energy, vibrating predominantly negatively or predominantly positively, yet all existing within the same universe. Those low negative beings in the spirit realm might *attempt* to manipulate and control your mind for attention. This is not something to be fearful of, but rather to be aware of, to ensure you are protected. No human or spirit can control you unless you allow it. Just as you use your own discernment with humans, you will naturally do the same with any spiritual encounters you may have.

The moment you choose to be fearful you allow your energy levels to enter a lower vibration. Therefore setting your positive intent, and trusting it, will be a good start to spiritual hygiene.

As you begin to meditate, your energy vibration will change. You bring all your energies and attention into your body to begin a physical and mental focus. This empowers your frequency and 'switches on the light', as viewed from the spiritual realm. Your energy is immediately brighter and more positive than in every-day life. All beings in the spiritual realm are ready and willing to take part. Your guides and all other positive, respectful beings are ready to feed you guidance and healing and to help and uplift your energies further, the moment you request and allow it. Requesting and allowing it is the key. The negative beings are disrespectful and ready to 'steal' some of your energy, wanting to manipulate or control you. You need to know that they truly cannot interfere with you unless you allow it. The difficult part of this process could be, are you *aware* of allowing interference? Are you aware of them controlling or manipulating you? The reason I teach the use of spiritual hygiene is for your safety, to protect you against being unaware. You can now drop all fear and allow yourself the wonderful and powerful experience of focused meditation.

Your spiritual guides assigned to helping you in your life can only do so much, and have to be invited by you to assist further. We all have a divine will and can choose to become involved with negative beings or positive beings. It is recommended that you do not meditate while under the influence of alcohol, drugs and sedative medications, as these substances automatically pull your energies into a low or negative vibration. Understand that whatever energy vibration you put out, you will attract the same to you. This is the natural law of attraction that operates in our universe. Therefore, your focus needs to be positive and clear for your own highest good. Praying regularly will shift your energies into a higher vibration and continue to increase it. So while your level of awareness is growing and developing, I strongly recommend the use of prayer to protect you at all times.

Begin all your meditations in a prayer-state of consciousness. I recommend the use of the following prayer before meditation, before going to sleep at night and on waking in the morning. It is a simple yet powerful form of day, and night, protection.

During the prayer, visualise yourself within a protective egg shape of white or gold light, whichever colour comes naturally to you.

Dear Mother/Father creator God of all there is, I ask for your presence, assistance, guidance and protection. I allow and invite my own spiritual guides, masters, angels and archangels to assist in my healing at this time, as in accordance with my Soul. I allow myself to absorb positive energies and always remain protected from any negative energy.

With this prayer you can trust you are protected, and will remain untouchable by any negative being, spiritual or physical.

On closing your meditation, you should pray again to give thanks and respect to all spiritual beings that were present and assisted you. I recommend the following prayer as a closure.

Dear Mother/Father creator God of all there is I give thanks for your presence, assistance, guidance and protection. I thank my own spiritual guides (use their name if you have it or their mental image if you have seen them), masters, angels and archangels, who assisted in my healing during this meditation.

Step 7 – Experience

Focus and visualise. Allow yourself to fully experience your meditation. Pay attention to all the thoughts, feelings and encounters you have.

Step 8 – Recall

Recall after your meditation is very important. By actively recalling your experience, you begin to develop a memory bridge. This too can increase your ability to remember your dreams while asleep. You can keep a meditation journal as well as a dream journal and record your experiences. By recalling your experiences, you can gain tremendous insight into yourself. You are going within when you meditate. The more you practice meditation, the more you will feel yourself entering a deeper level. You will be actively training your brain-waves to enter into, and stay, in the theta wave.

Easy meditations for beginners

The easiest way to start with focused meditations is through your senses and relaxation. I love working with the senses as they rapidly open up awareness levels. Practice any one or more daily. You can read through the short ones and then do it from memory. For the longer meditations, I recommend you read it out loud and record it, or download the recordings available on www.tinacornish.co.za. This way you can listen to it often. Listening to recorded meditations can help you to remain in a relaxed focus state so you can achieve the theta brain-wave. You can also use the Relaxation Meditation as an introduction to all your meditations to help ensure your body is relaxed. With practice, you will discover your body relaxing quickly and easily. After regular practice, you will be able to do away with a long relaxation start to your meditation, as your body will be trained to relax quickly.

To recap on your steps to follow:
1. Stretching
2. Posture
3. Intention
4. Grounding
5. Breathing
6. Spiritual Hygiene (prayer and protection)
7. Experience
8. Recall

Relaxation for Stress Relief – Meditation

Use this to learn how to relax your body for meditations and to release stress.

Stretch your body and breathe in deeply. Sit back and ensure you are comfortable. Arms and legs must be uncrossed, feet comfortable on the floor. Palms facing up. Close your eyes and focus your intention on relaxing. Begin to relax your body into the chair. Feel a golden beam of energy flowing through the crown of your head, right through your body, down and out the soles of your feet. Allow the golden beam of energy to go deep into the core of earth and connect to a pink rose quartz crystal. Just settle with this energy of connection running through you. Feel your breathing becoming deep, calm and peaceful. Imagine a pure, white, egg shape of energy all around you for protection.

Be Aware

Dear Mother/Father creator God of all there is, I ask for your presence, assistance, guidance and protection. I allow and invite my own spiritual guides, masters, angels and archangels to assist in my healing at this time, as in accordance with my Soul. I allow myself to absorb positive energies and remain protected against any negative energy.

Breathe in deeply to the count of three, hold in to the count of three, and exhale out very slowly. Breathe in again: hold one, two, three; exhale very slowly. Breathe in deeply, one, two, three; hold in, one, two, three; exhale very slowly. Focus on each area by tightening and releasing. Shift your focus to the soles of your feet. Feel your feet connecting to the ground. Relax your toes, move up to the top of your foot. Concentrate on your ankles, your shins; tighten your calves and release. Relax your knees. Tighten your thighs and release; tighten your butt and relax. Tighten your lower stomach area and feel the release; move up to just below your ribs, tightening and releasing as you move up. Feel the inside of your abdomen relaxing. Relax your chest, your shoulders. Tighten your upper arms and release; your lower arms and release; and, without making a fist, tighten your hands and release. Relax your neck, feel the release travelling down your spine. Enjoy it. Now feel the release travel up your spine to the base of your head. Move the energy, over your head from the back to the front; release it. Relax your jaw, your tongue, your throat, your ears, your cheeks. Stretch your nose down and release; release your eyes and brow. Your body is now completely relaxed. Silently say thank-you to your body for all its hard work. Spend some time sensing how your body feels now. Just be one with it.

Concentrating on your breathing, slowly deepen each breath. Stretch your fingers and toes; stretch your body. Take in a deep breath and exhale slowly.

Dear Mother/Father creator God of all there is I give thanks for your presence, assistance, guidance and protection. I thank my own spiritual guides, masters, angels and archangels, who assisted in my healing during this meditation.

When you feel ready, you may slowly open your eyes. Stretch your body and recall your meditation.

Senses Meditation – Smell

Begin with the basic techniques of steps 1-7. Spend 5 to 10 minutes with your eyes closed and focus on any fragrance you prefer. Imagine breathing it in, allowing it right into your brain and flowing through your body. Allow any thoughts or visions that come with this fragrance, being alert to whether this feels good to you or not. You can also have a fragrance present to assist you. Example: hold an orange, smell it, before you close your eyes. Close your meditation in prayer. Complete step 8 (Recall).

Senses Meditation – Taste

Begin with the basic techniques of steps 1-7. Spend 5 to 10 minutes with your eyes closed and focus on any taste you can recall. Take yourself through various tastes: sweetness, bitterness, salty, sour. Be alert to whether this feels good to you or not. Close your meditation in prayer. Complete step 8 (Recall).

Senses Meditation – Hear

Begin with the basic techniques of steps 1-7. Spend 5 to 10 minutes with your eyes closed and focus on any sounds and tones you may hear around you. There are always sounds around us, even in the most peaceful environments. Become aware of vibrations that come with the various tones. Listen to the sound of the birds singing. If the sound is coming from a source close to you, you will be able to feel the vibration with concentration. Electricity, having a negative impact on our energies, can easily be heard, especially from fluorescent lights and computers. Connect with the tones and feel their impact as they vibrate through your body. Be alert to whether this feels good to you or not. Close your meditation in prayer. Complete step 8 (Recall).

Senses Meditation – Touch
Begin with the basic techniques of steps 1-7. Spend 5 to 10 minutes with your eyes closed and focus on your clothes touching your skin. Your body on the chair. The different fabrics. Connect with and feel the various touches vibrating through your body, being alert to whether this feels good to you or not. Close your meditation in prayer. Complete step 8 (Recall).

Senses Meditation – Sight
Begin with the basic techniques of steps 1-7. Spend 5 to 10 minutes with your eyes closed and see and imagine any colour filling your entire body and energy (auric) field around you. Just remain present in this colour, and allow any other colour that comes your way to do so. Allow yourself to truly feel the vibration that comes along with colour, being alert to whether this feels good to you or not. What else do you see? Close your meditation in prayer. Complete step 8 (Recall).

The Walking, Talking, Living – Meditation
In your everyday life, bring in the use of any or all of the above senses and meditate with your eyes open.

My favourite is making use of nature. If you do not have a garden, visit your local nursery and enjoy the many different healthy plants. Be aware of your feet on the ground as you walk around. Reach out and touch a plant gently. Feel the tickle on your hand. Smell the fragrance of the flowers. Absorb the colour of the flowers and green leaves. Touch the soil. Feel the sturdy stem. Allow yourself to communicate silently with the plant. Express your gratitude and show your respect as it, too, is a living source in this universe.

Release Problems through Love – Meditation

Use this meditation to release any problems.

Stretch your body and breathe in deeply. Sit back and ensure you are comfortable. Arms and legs must be uncrossed; feet comfortable on the floor. Palms facing up. Close your eyes and focus your intention on Love. Begin to relax your body into the chair. Feel a golden beam of energy flowing through the crown of your head, right through your body, down and out the soles of your feet. Allow the golden beam of energy to go deep into the core of the earth and connect to a pink rose quartz crystal. Just settle with this energy of connection running through you. Feel your breathing becoming deep, calm and peaceful. Imagine a pure, white, egg shape of energy all around you for protection.

Dear Mother/Father creator God of all there is, I ask for your presence, assistance, guidance and protection. I allow and invite my own spiritual guides, masters, angels and archangels to assist in my healing at this time, as in accordance with my Soul. I allow myself to absorb positive energies and remain protected against any negative energy.

Breathe in deeply to the count of three, hold in to the count of three, and exhale very slowly. Breathe in again: hold in, one, two, three;

exhale very slowly. Breathe in deeply, one, two, three; hold in, one, two, three; exhale very slowly. Focus on each area by tightening and releasing. Shift your focus to the soles of your feet. Feel your feet connecting to the ground. Relax your toes, move up to the top of your foot. Concentrate on your ankles, your shins; tighten your calves and release. Relax your knees. Tighten your thighs and release, tighten your butt and relax. Tighten your lower stomach area and feel the release; move up to just below your ribs, tightening and releasing as you move up. Feel the inside of your abdomen relaxing. Relax your chest, your shoulders. Tighten your upper arms and release; your lower arms and release; and without making a fist, tighten your hands and release. Relax your neck, feel the release travelling down your spine. Enjoy it. Now feel the release travel up your spine to the base of your head. Move the energy over your head, from the back to the front and release it. Relax your jaw, your tongue, your throat, your ears, your cheeks. Stretch your nose down and release; release your eyes and brow. Your body is now completely relaxed. Silently say thank-you to your body for all its hard work.

Imagine you are in a powerful, bright, golden ball of energy. All of God's love and light fills this golden energy around you. Allow yourself to absorb this energy into your body; through your skin, through your breathing. Focus on your heart, see deep within, and listen to the sound of your own heartbeat. See a violet and pink bubble of light right in the centre of your heart. This bubble is pure, divine, loving energy already born deep inside of you. It has always been there and can never leave you. Keep focus on this violet and pink bubble and feel the love that it radiates within you. Watch as this bubble begins to expand. As you focus on it, it grows bigger, filling you with an abundance of divine love. Let it expand throughout your whole body; see the violet and pink energy swirling all around you. With this love comes peace, serenity, happiness, joy, fulfilment, laughter, compassion, empathy, understanding, forgiveness. Absorb all these energies. Feel your whole body uplifting and changing as you continue to focus on this loving energy. Extend the bubble outside your body, surrounding you. Take in a deeper breath of God's pure, divine golden energy. Let it come in through the crown of your head. Allow this golden energy to filter through your entire body and into your surrounding violet and pink bubble. Allow any part of your body that is out of balance or currently ill to absorb more of this energy to bring about healing. With the focus of the energy bubble outside of your body, bring into your thoughts any problems you are having in your life at this moment. Allow this loving energy to surround the problem; to filter into the core of the problem; and to heal this problem in accordance with the highest good intentions of your own Soul. Now see this problem ascending in one of its own golden bubbles. Allow it to leave, to be taken care of by God or any of the celestial beings who are currently with you, for healing. Focus again on the bubble around you. What does this feel like now, do you feel lighter and freer? If there are more problems you need to let go of right now, continue to allow them to ascend.

How do you feel now? More relaxed, freer, and lighter? Keep yourself in this bubble of violet and pink energy surrounded by gold. Concentrating on your breathing, slowly deepen each breath. Stretch your fingers and toes; stretch your body. Take in a deep breath and exhale slowly.

Dear Mother/Father creator God of all there is I give thanks for your presence, assistance, guidance and protection. I thank my own spiritual guides, masters, angels and archangels, who assisted in my healing during this meditation.

When you feel ready, you may slowly open your eyes.

Connect with your guides and guardians – Meditation

Use this meditation to connect with your spirit guides and guardian angels.

Stretch your body and breathe in deeply. Sit back and ensure you are comfortable. Arms and legs must be uncrossed; feet comfortable on the floor. Palms face up. Close your eyes and focus your intention on connecting to your guides. Begin to relax your body into the chair. Feel a golden beam of energy flowing through the crown of your head, right through your body, and down out the soles of your feet. Allow the golden beam of energy to go deep into the core of the earth and connect to a pink rose quartz crystal. Just settle with this energy of connection running through you. Feel your breathing becoming deep, calm and peaceful. Imagine a pure, white, egg shape of energy all around you for protection.

Dear Mother/Father creator God of all there is, I ask for your presence, assistance, guidance and protection. I allow and invite my own spiritual guides, masters, angels and archangels to assist in my healing at this time, as in accordance with my Soul. I allow myself to absorb positive energies and remain protected against any negative energy.

Breathe in deeply to the count of three, hold in to the count of three, and exhale very slowly. Breathe in again: hold in, one, two, three; exhale very slowly. Breathe in deeply, one, two, three; hold in, one, two, three; exhale very slowly. Focus on each area by tightening and releasing. Shift your focus to the soles of your feet. Feel your feet connecting to the ground. Relax your toes, move up to the top of your foot. Concentrate on your ankles, your shins; tighten your calves and release. Relax your knees. Tighten your thighs and release; tighten your butt and relax. Tighten your lower stomach area and feel the release; move up to just below your ribs, tightening and releasing as you move up. Feel the inside of your abdomen relaxing. Relax your chest, your shoulders. Tighten your upper arms and release; your lower arms and release; and, without making a fist, tighten your hands and release. Relax your neck, feel the release travelling down your spine. Enjoy it. Now feel the release travel up your spine to the base of your head. Move the energy over your head, from the back to the front; release it. Relax your jaw, your tongue, your throat, your ears, your cheeks. Stretch your nose down and release; release your eyes and brow. Your body is now completely relaxed. Silently say thank-you to your body for all its hard work.

Imagine you are in a powerful, bright, golden ball of energy. All of God's love and light fills this golden energy around you. Allow yourself to absorb this energy into your body; through your skin, through your breathing. Focus on your heart, see deep within, and listen to the sound of your own heartbeat. Ask your spirit guide to come forward, please show yourself to me. What is your name? Allow yourself to feel, see, hear or sense the reply. What is your purpose in my life? Feel, see, hear or sense the reply. Ask your guardian angel to come forward, please show yourself to me. What is your name? Allow yourself to feel, see, hear or sense the reply. What is your purpose in my life? Feel, see, hear or sense the reply. Allow yourself quiet time to receive. Communicate with them. Feel relaxed and peaceful. Thank them for connecting and communicating with you.

Concentrating on your breathing, slowly deepen each breath. Stretch your fingers and toes; stretch your body. Take in a deep breath and exhale slowly.

Dear Mother/Father creator God of all there is I give thanks for your presence, assistance, guidance and protection. I thank my own spiritual guides, masters, angels and archangels, who assisted in my healing during this meditation.

When you feel ready, you may slowly open your eyes.

Connect with your Soul – Meditation

Use this meditation to connect with your Soul.

Stretch your body and breathe in deeply. Sit back and ensure you are comfortable. Arms and legs must be uncrossed; feet comfortable on the floor. Palms facing up. Close your eyes and focus your intention on connecting to your Soul. Begin to relax your body into the chair. Feel a golden beam of energy flowing through the crown of your head, right through your body, down and out the soles of your feet. Allow the golden beam of energy to go deep into the core of the earth and connect to a pink rose quartz crystal. Just settle with this energy of connection running through you. Feel your breathing becoming deep, calm and peaceful. Imagine a pure, white, egg shape of energy all around you for protection.

Dear Mother/Father creator God of all there is, I ask for your presence, assistance, guidance and protection. I allow and invite my own spiritual guides, masters, angels and archangels to assist in my healing at this time, as in accordance with my Soul. I allow myself to absorb positive energies and remain protected against any negative energy.

Breathe in deeply to the count of three, hold in to the count of three, and exhale very slowly. Breathe in again: hold in, one, two, three; exhale very slowly. Breathe in deeply, one, two, three; hold in, one, two, three; exhale very slowly. Focus on each area by tightening and releasing. Shift your focus to the soles of your feet. Feel your feet connecting to the ground. Relax your toes, move up to the top of your foot. Concentrate on your ankles, your shins; tighten your calves and release. Relax your

242

knees. Tighten your thighs and release; tighten your butt and relax. Tighten your lower stomach area and feel the release; move up to just below your ribs, tightening and releasing as you move up. Feel the inside of your abdomen relaxing. Relax your chest, your shoulders. Tighten your upper arms and release; your lower arms and release; and without making a fist, tighten your hands and release. Relax your neck, feel the release travelling down your spine. Enjoy it. Now feel the release travel up your spine to the base of your head. Move the energy over your head, from the back to the front; release it. Relax your jaw, your tongue, your throat, your ears, your cheeks. Stretch your nose down and release; release your eyes and brow. Your body is now completely relaxed. Silently say thank-you to your body for all its hard work.

Imagine you are in a powerful, bright, golden ball of energy. All of God's love and light fills this golden energy around you. Allow yourself to absorb this energy into your body; through your skin, through your breathing. Focus on your heart, see deep within, and listen to the sound of your own heartbeat. Ask your spirit guide or guardian angel to help you connect to your Soul. Feel the lightness as you connect. See how expanded your Soul is. How do you feel? Sense your pure and magnificent vibration. Perhaps there is a colour of your Soul. What is it? Feel connected and at one with your Soul. Ask your Soul, what am I to do in this life? Feel, sense or hear the answer. How can I accomplish it? Feel, sense or hear the answer. Allow time to be. Completely connect to your Soul. Be completely aware of the vibrational communication.

Feel relaxed, peaceful and satisfied. Thank your Soul for being with you at all times, for communicating with you.

Concentrating on your breathing, slowly deepen each breath. Stretch your fingers and toes; stretch your body. Take in a deep breath and exhale slowly.

Dear Mother/Father creator God of all there is I give thanks for your presence, assistance, guidance and protection. I thank my own spiritual guides, masters, angels and archangels, who assisted in my healing during this meditation.

When you feel ready, you may slowly open your eyes.

Crystal Healing Cave – Meditation

Use this meditation for any releasing and healing you require.

Stretch your body and breathe in deeply. Sit back and ensure you are comfortable. Arms and legs must be uncrossed; feet comfortable on the floor. Palms facing up. Close your eyes and focus your intention on receiving healing. Begin to relax your body. Feel a golden beam of energy flowing through the crown of your head, right through your body, down and out the soles of your feet. Allow the golden beam of energy to go deep into the core of the earth and connect to a pink rose quartz crystal. Just settle with this energy of connection running through you.

Dear Mother/Father creator God of all there is, I ask for your presence, assistance, guidance and protection. I allow and invite my own spiritual guides, masters, angels and archangels to assist in my healing at this time, as in accordance with my Soul. I allow myself to absorb positive energies and remain protected against any negative energy.

Breathe in deeply to the count of three, hold in to the count of three; and exhale very slowly. Breathe in again: hold in, one, two, three; exhale very slowly. Breathe in deeply, one, two, three; hold in, one, two, three; exhale very slowly. Focus on each area by tightening and releasing.

Shift your focus to the soles of your feet. Feel your feet connecting to the ground. Relax your toes, move up to the top of your foot. Concentrate on your ankles, your shins; tighten your calves and release. Relax your knees. Tighten your thighs and release; tighten your butt and relax. Tighten your lower stomach area, and feel the release; move up to just below your ribs, tightening and releasing as you move up. Feel the inside of your abdomen relaxing. Relax your chest, your shoulders. Tighten your upper arms and release; your lower arms and release; and without making a fist, tighten your hands and release. Relax your neck, feel the release travelling down your spine. Enjoy it. Now feel the release travel up your spine to the base of your head. Move the energy over your head, from the back to the front; release it. Relax your jaw, your tongue, your throat, your ears, your cheeks. Stretch your nose down and release; release your eyes and brow. Your body is now completely relaxed. Silently say thank-you to your body for all its hard work.

Allow yourself to gentle float off on a special and sacred journey to the Himalayas. Float up high over Mount Everest. Below you, peeking through the misty clouds, are snow-covered mountains. Float on over two rivers, a crystal blue and an aquamarine green river. They join together and form rapids as they cascade down the mountain. Gently descend over the joined river just after the rapids. Beside the river are large rocks of jasper and granite. The jasper rocks are red, with glistening speckles of golden sunlight dancing over them. Gently float down and stand on the jasper rocks. Take off your shoes and feel the warmth penetrating your feet. Allow the jasper to induce your body into a state of healing and rebirth. Be aware of how all your senses open while connected to the jasper. Take a couple of steps down off the rocks and enter into the crisp, clear, blue-green and pristine water. Feel its coolness against your skin.

You are comfortable and relaxed in this water. Walk deeper, feeling the water becoming warmer. Know that this water carries powerful healing energies just for you to enjoy right now. Submerge yourself in this water and feel completely safe, relax on your back and allow any fears, anxieties or depression to slowly emerge. Acknowledge your thoughts and feelings, allow them to be washed and cleansed with this healing water. Hear the distant sound of rapids in the river. Feel the vibration from the rapids as they slowly and gentle ripple over your body. Above you, silently and peacefully, the mountain mist is passing by. Connect to the clouds as they effortlessly move by. Feeling cleansed and free, slowly walk out of this river and sit on the jasper rocks. Absorb the warmth of the jasper under your feet and bum. Allow the high, penetrating sun to dry and warm you. Stand and turn to your left. Walk along the nearby pathway. Absorb the energy from the natural vegetation growing along-side this path. Allow all your senses to open; smell, see and hear. Listen to the sound of your footprints and the distant sound of the rapids. Feel the sacred energies rising from this land, up through the soles of your feet and into your body. The energy is helping you to feel inspired and relaxed. In front of you is a cave, completely surrounded by gold; feel the power of this gold radiating towards you as you walk into the cave. As you enter, feel the sound vibration changing around you. Your ears are alert. Through the quiet stillness, hear a very high-pitched tone that creates a soothing vibration. Smell the sweet smell of jasmine and any other fragrance that you are aware of. Notice the further reduction of light as you continue walking deep within. Be aware of the light vanishing behind you as you walk deeper into the darkness. In front of you are three golden steps glowing and welcoming you. Walk down them into the heart of this cave. Cast your eyes across to see and feel the beauty and brightness that is ahead of you. Walk on into it. The bright light now surrounds you. Vibrant crystals completely cover the walls. Each and every crystal carries its own vibrational sound and healing frequency. This is the high-pitched and soothing tone you can hear. The full spectrum of bright colours radiating from these crystals vibrate their beams forward to unite in the heart of this cave. Feel the magnificence of all these crystal beams vibrating all around you. In the middle point, many celestial beings stand and wait prepared for your arrival. Your spirit guides, guardian angels, ascended masters, archangels, all gathered just for you. Greet them and feel the love, comfort and security they project towards you now. There is a soft, feather-filled mattress welcoming you. Your guardian angel comes forth, takes your hand and guides you to the mattress. Climb on and lie down. Feel your body relaxing deep into the softness. All the celestial beings move forward and surround you. Each of them comes, one by one, takes your hand and introduces themselves to you. Now standing around you, feel their light, soft hands, gently being placed upon all areas of your body. Feel their love and light penetrate your body as gentle, pulsating waves of heat. Allow yourself to go with the flow of this healing for your highest good. Above you, notice there is a strong powerful beam of golden loving energy coming directly from the sun, through an opening at the top of the cave. See this golden energy connecting to the crystal beams, empowering every crystal in the walls and every celestial being present with you. Know that all this is pure, golden, divine love and light from the sun. It is sent forward by God to heal you in the most powerful and miraculous way you can imagine. Allow yourself to totally absorb all this energy, love and light. Let any thoughts or feelings rise up and out of you now. It is your time to let go and heal yourself. Feel comfortable to cry if tears arise. Let go of all problems and obstacles in your life. Completely allow yourself to go with the flow of any thought or feeling that comes up. This is what you are ready to let go of now. Repeat silently to yourself, *I forgive myself, I love myself, and I allow myself to learn from my past lessons. I love and forgive others too.* See and feel yourself moving through this phase until total peace comes over you. Know that all you need to release has been released. Silently ask God and the celestial beings to ensure all your patterns and energy cords connected to these past events, thoughts, and feelings, be effectively released. That the energy cords be cut and cleared. Ask that any karmic ties to others be cut and released. Now feel the vibration increasing within you as all cords are cut. Feel the release. The golden energies from above are now entering each and every cell in your body, going deep into your DNA. Healing and cleansing for your highest good. All negative thought patterns and illnesses are cleared for you. Relax and absorb the energy of all your guides and angels around you. Connect and communicate with them. What messages do they have? As your healing comes to an end, thank all the celestial beings for their love, light and healing. Feel yourself becoming lighter and lifting directly up into God's bright golden beam of light as you ascend through the top of this cave and out into the beautiful blue sky. Remaining enveloped in God's golden love and light, float back to where your physical body is. Feel yourself, comfortable now in your body; safe, secure and filled with love and peace.

Concentrating on your breathing, slowly deepen each breath. Stretch your fingers and toes; stretch your body. Take in a deep breath and exhale slowly.

Dear Mother/Father creator God of all there is I give thanks for your presence, assistance, guidance and protection. I thank my own spiritual guides, masters, angels and archangels, who assisted in my healing during this meditation.

When you feel ready, you may slowly open your eyes.

Archangels – Meditation

Use this meditation to connect with a team of archangels to help you in life and prepare you for your ascension.

Stretch your body and breathe in deeply. Sit back and ensure you are comfortable. Arms and legs must be uncrossed; feet comfortable on the floor. Palms facing up. Close your eyes and focus your intention on connecting with archangels. Begin to relax your body. Feel a golden beam of energy flowing through the crown of your head, right through your body, and down out the soles of your feet. Allow the golden beam of energy to go deep into the core of the earth and connect to a pink rose quartz crystal. Just settle with this energy of connection running through you.

Dear Mother/Father creator God of all there is, I ask for your presence, assistance, guidance and protection. I allow and invite my own spiritual guides, masters, angels to assist in my connection to the archangels at this time, as in accordance with my Soul. Please send forth Archangels Michael, Jophiel, Chamuel, Uriel, Gabriel, Raphael, Zadkiel and Metatron.

Archangel Michael, place your deep to royal blue with purple red sparkles cloak of protection around me. Infuse me with your power, faith, courage and divine will, aligning me into my Soul life purpose. Please ensure I become consciously aware of what I need to do. Be still and silent as you feel Archangel Michael around you now. Hear the vibration and communicate.

Be Aware

Archangel Jophiel, illuminate my mind with your wisdom, intelligence and insight. Guide my thoughts and ideas. Fill and infuse your yellow energy into mine. Guide me forth into the wisdom of my Soul. Be still and silent as you feel Archangel Jophiel around you now. Hear the vibration and communicate.

Archangel Chamuel, fill me with your deep pink energy of love and compassion. Help me to share this love and compassion with everyone I am in contact with. Be still and silent as you feel Archangel Chamuel around you now. Hear the vibration and communicate.

Archangel Gabriel, send forth your white vibration all around and within me. Infuse me with your joy and purity. Help me remain disciplined in connecting and communicating truthfully. Be still and silent as you feel Archangel Gabriel around you now. Hear the vibration and communicate.

Archangel Raphael, please shower me with your green light. Guide me to avoid all toxic foods and beverages that are harmful for my body. Show me the healthy foods and beverages I can consume, those that help me to keep my body vibrating strong and healthy. Be still and silent as you feel Archangel Raphael around you now. Hear the vibration and communicate.

Archangel Uriel, fill me with your peace and harmony, help me to deal with my emotions as they arise and not suppress them within my body to create future illnesses. Be still and silent as you feel and see deep gold with purple, blue and ruby flecks of Archangel Uriel around you now. Hear the vibration and communicate.

Archangel Zadkiel, blaze your deep violet flame of light within, keeping me in freedom and tolerance, helping me to forgive and release whenever situations arise, helping me to remain with an open heart, filled with love. Be still and silent as you feel Archangel Zadkiel around you now. Hear the vibration and communicate.

Archangel Metraton, fill me with your golden orange and silver light. Send your metatronic cube of light and wisdom down through my crown and to all my chakras. Help prepare my body for ascension and guide me forth from here on. Show me where and how I can help you with children or adults on our earth. Be still and silent as you feel Archangel Metatron around you now. Hear the vibration and communicate.

Feel all Archangels Michael, Jophiel, Chamuel, Uriel, Gabriel, Raphael, Zadkiel and Metatron standing around you. *I ask all of you to help me connect and communicate with each of you more often. Show me where in my life I can make changes. Help me to be of more service to others. Thank you, I appreciate your presence, healing and guidance.*

Dear Mother/Father creator God of all that is. I give thanks and appreciation for your presence love and acceptance. I thank the archangels, my spiritual guides and angels. In love, light and gratitude, Amen.

Slowly open your eyes and stretch your body.

Afterword

This book and journey of my life has been an amazing healing and awakening experience that transformed me into who I am today. May your life become your greatest healing, awakening and transformational process for you? Go with the flow of your life. Do not be rigid and inflexible. Your life is divinely guided. Value it and appreciate every experience you go through. I know your life will change too after reading this book.

Open your heart and mind. Listen to all the messages coming your way from all different mediums. You, too, are awakening right now. Let us all unite in conscious awareness and ascend into whatever higher dimension we each choose.

I now leave *my moments of awareness* in your hands with a question for you.

"What are you going to *BE NOW*?"

I share these words from an ancient and wise man, recorded in 'Super Memory', by Douglas J Herrmann.

"May you always remember what is important and forget the rest."

If you have been inspired, gained healing or any other form of transformation through my book in any way, please contact me via www.tinacornish.co.za I look forward to hearing from you.

"Always remember, you are more than you think you are right now. You are forever growing wiser, changing in body, mind and spirit. Never forget your own power to just BE!" Love and Light, Tina Cornish.

Bibliography

Bays Brandon The Journey [Book]. - Great Britain : Thorsons, 1999.

Brennan Barbara Ann Light Emerging - The Journey of Personal Healing [Book]. - United States and Canada : Bantam Doubleday Dell Publishing, 1993.

Hay Louise L. Heal Your Body [Book]. - United States of America : Hay House, 1988.

Herrmann Douglas J. Super Memory [Book]. - Great Britain : Blandford, 1995.

Inserra Rose Dictionary of Dreams [Book]. - Australia : Hinkler Books, 2002.

Oxford University Press The Concise Oxford Dictionary of Current English [Book]. - England : Oxford University Press, 1991.

Virtue Doreen The Care and Feeding of Indigo Children [Book]. - United States of America : Hay House, 2001.

About the Author

Tina Cornish, a Reiki Master since 2003 and a Self-proclaimed Coach, is working with God, a team of Archangels and Ascended Masters to bring forth an ever-expanding higher dimensional energy to assist humanity to transform their own consciousness through the Christ-light field. She helps you to understand and translate the universal divine order already taking place in your life. Tina is passionate about empowering you to heal, and transform, with love and appreciation for your life. She is certified in Colour Therapy, Communication Skills, Merkaba Meditation and has also studied and used Crystals, Meridian Therapy, EFT (Emotional Freedom Techniques) and Feng Shui. She was born in Zimbabwe and resides in South Africa. She is a wife and mom of two.